DISCOVER SCOTLAND'S WILDLIFE

Photographs by Ged Connelly
and other wildlife photographers

Written by Rosalind Jones

Designed by Susan MacKinnon
Maps by Wendy Price Cartographic Services
Printed by Clunie Group Limited, Oban, Argyll.

Published in aid of the Scottish Wildlife Trust
With sponsorship from Forestry Commission Scotland and Wild Scotland

Craigmore Publications www.craigmore-publications.co.uk

DISCOVER SCOTLAND'S WILDLIFE

Have you ever seen an otter eating its catch by a deserted loch, or watched majestic eagles soaring overhead? Have you ever spotted deer silhouetted against the skyline, or been captivated by the antics of red squirrels? Watching dolphins performing acrobatics; comical puffins disappearing into cliff-top burrows; whales lunging hungrily at fish shoals; gannets plunging – wings folded into the waves, are magnificent sights you could see. Maybe you might like to quietly observe rare dragonflies and butterflies in a meadow, or discover the 'world within a world' of a rock pool on one of Scotland's seashores? These and other fascinating wildlife experiences await you if you visit the right places or join a guided wildlife tour. The British Isles have the richest and most diverse wildlife in Europe; and Scotland with its wealth of wild natural environments is Britain's foremost wildlife haven.

'Discover Scotland's Wildlife' is an introduction to Scotland's extra special mammals, birds, and other wildlife uniquely found here or present in greater numbers than anywhere else in Britain. Of course there are hundreds of other birds and animals to be seen as well! A map, pin-pointing locations of wildlife venues and guided tours, plus a directory with contact numbers and websites will help you plan where to go and what you could see. Most venues are run by wildlife or environmental charities including The Royal Society for the Protection of Birds (RSPB), The National Trust for Scotland (NTS) or government agencies: the Forestry Commission for Scotland (FCS) and Scottish Natural Heritage (SNH). Other activities are organised by local landowners or companies. All venues and visitor centres are dedicated to the enjoyment of Scotland's natural assets as well as raising awareness about the challenges faced by Scotland's wildlife.

This book aims to help raise awareness of the wealth of wildlife to be discovered and enjoyed and it has been published in support of the Scottish Wildlife Trust – a charity dedicated to wildlife conservation. All profits from its sale will be donated to assist their conservation and awareness-raising work.

Over 120 wildlife reserves are managed by the Scottish Wildlife Trust (SWT) which is also involved in a project that aims to bring back beavers to Scotland. Once native, beavers were hunted to extinction in Scotland during the 16th century. Beavers are known as keystone species because their presence improves habitats and benefits other species. To regain their positive effect on these environments and to assist the biodiversity of wetlands and woodlands, beavers are to be reintroduced on a trial basis into Knapdale Forest, Mid-Argyll, by SWT working together with the Royal Zoological Society of Scotland.

Special thanks are due to the photographers who have provided superb images which, in themselves, show a great appreciation of Scotland's natural wealth. These photos will help you identify what you discover, whilst eleven factual short stories, encompassing a variety of Scotland's wildlife, will take you into their fascinating worlds as you experience a day, or more, of their lives. With woodlands, peatlands, grassland, uplands, seashores, and islands, you have many wonderful environments to discover and explore. The photographers and the writer hope to introduce you to the fantastic 'wild side' of Scotland, to provide you with a souvenir to take home with you and to encourage you to enjoy wildlife experiences in Scotland that you will never forget.

There are hundreds of wildlife venues to visit but, if you have never watched wildlife before or if time is limited and you want to be rewarded with sightings then join one of the many wildlife trips, either day 'safaris' on land or sea trips, many of which specialise in watching marine mammals, especially cetaceans. Be sure to go with a guide who respects the SNH Marine Code or a member of 'WiSe', the UK's first wildlife-friendly accreditation scheme for marine tour organisers. Both aim to reduce disturbance and promote safe observation of wildlife.

Many visitors to Scotland hope to see 'Nessie', the 'Loch Ness Monster' first noted by St. Columba 14 centuries ago. Even more elusive than sightings of 'Nessie' are those of the now very rare, endangered, Scottish wildcat. Visitors to the West Coast feel privileged to encounter flocks of magnificent, silky coated, scimitar-horned 'wild goats', the feral descendants of domestic goats. Many, however, will proudly take home photos of golden shaggy, sweeping horned Highland cattle that are wild-looking but usually docile!

Scotland has long been famed for its hunting and fishing but today more and more discerning visitors arrive with cameras to 'shoot' and 'capture' Scotland's wildlife. The modern emphasis is now on conservation and appreciation. 'DISCOVER SCOTLAND'S WILDLIFE' has been produced with this ideal in mind. All those involved in the production of this publication hope you will enjoy it.

*The Scottish Wildlife Trust is the largest voluntary body working for all the wildlife of Scotland. It represents more than 30,000 members who care for wildlife and the environment and manages over 120 reserves across Scotland including three visitor centres. SWT seeks to raise public awareness of threatened habitats and species, and, as a registered charity, relies on public donations. You can help Scotland's wildlife even more by becoming a member or by giving a donation. Visit **www.swt.org.uk**. email: enquiries@swt.org.uk or telephone 0131 312 7765 for more information.*

The Scottish Wildlife Trust is a company limited by guarantee, registered in Scotland (registration number SC040247) having its registered office at Cramond House, Cramond Glebe Road, Edinburgh EH4 6NS. It is also a Scottish registered charity (Charity number SC005792).

DISCOVER SCOTLAND'S AQUATIC MAMMALS

Minke Whale, *Balaenoptera acutorostrata* has the Gaelic name muc-mara, meaning 'sea pig'. The minke is also known as: least finner, little piked whale, pikehead, sharp-headed finner, or lesser rorqual. Adult females grow up to 9.1m and adult males to 8.8m. Their average weight at sexual maturity is 4–5 tonnes. Gestation of young is 10 months, and they become mature in 7–8 years. They can live up to 60 years.

Killer Whale, *Orcinus orca*, often known simply as 'Orca'. Patterned black and white, they are a top predator with a diverse diet, feeding on large fish, seals, and even dolphins. Playful and inquisitive they live in long term social groups of up to 50 individuals. Males have a tall dorsal fin up to 1.9m in height. Females have a smaller, curved dorsal fin half this size.

Harbour Porpoise, *Phocoena phocoena* has a Gaelic name that translates as 'puffing pig' because the noise of their blow is often heard before they are seen. They live in shallow coastal waters and are often seen from the land in groups of 2–5 individuals. Dark grey in colour, males grow to 1.8m and females to 1.9m. Harbour porpoises have a varied diet of fish, shrimps, and squid but are threatened by being caught in fishing nets, and pollution.

Common Dolphin, *Delphinus delphis*, are seen all over the world, travelling in groups of 10–500. Sometimes known as White-sided dolphins because of distinctive white and cream patterns on their sides, they have beaked noses and are noisy, acrobatic, and graceful. They grow up to 2.5m.

Bottlenose Dolphin, *Tursiops truncates*, are renowned for their gymnastic displays of leaping and splashing alongside boats. Their rounded bodies are mostly grey in colour with a white underside, a curved dorsal fin, pointed flippers, and a protruding 'beak-like' head. They can grow up to 3.8m and travel in pods of males, females and calves.

Atlantic or Grey Seal, *Halichoerus grypus*, grey with large spots, have bulbous eyes, thick wrinkled necks, and a long muzzle. They grow up to 2.5m and with a diet of 5–6kg of fish daily they can weigh 250kg or more. Pups are born with white fur and weigh around 14kg. Males can live for 25 years, females for around 35 years. When eating, they often just take one bite from a fish and then discard it.

Common or Harbour Seal, *Phoca vitrulina*, have grey or brown fur patterned with fine spots. Around half the size of grey seals they weigh at most 130kg, feeding on herring, sand eels, whiting and crustaceans. Solitary when in the water they gather in groups or rookeries when they haul out on beaches or rocks. Pups, which can swim from birth, are born with adult colouring and grow fast on their mother's rich fatty milk.

Otter, *Lutra lutra*, are playful, streamlined, sleek but well-built aquatic animals that nest on land. Males typically weigh 10–12kg and measure up to 120cms, females are about two-thirds a males size and weight. Both have very sharp canines and strong crushing molars enabling then to crunch fish bones and shellfish. Males have territories extending 20 kilometres, females half that. Their favourite food is eels.

Minke Whale

Killer Whale

Harbour Porpoise

Common Dolphin

Bottlenose Dolphin

Atlantic Seal

Common Seal

Otter

DISCOVER SCOTLAND'S LAND MAMMALS

Pine Marten, *Martes martes*, are lithe chocolate brown, yellow-throated coloured carnivores growing up to 80cm in length. Once common coniferous forest dwellers their best stronghold is in the Caledonian pine forests of northern Scotland. Elusive and mainly nocturnal their diet consists of field voles, mice, rabbits, songbirds, frogs and beetles.

Badger, *Meles meles*, are nocturnal, clean living woodland animals that live in social groups, maintaining their extensively burrowed underground homes, called setts, in pristine order. Disliked by farmers because they carry bovine tuberculosis they are in fact the farmer's friend because they eat baby rabbits, voles, slugs, grass snakes, beetles, bees and wasps nests, fungi, as well as earthworms (as many as 250 per night). They don't hibernate but in winter may become dormant for several days.

Red Fox, *Vulpes vulpes*, are agile, lithe, reddish brown dog-like mammals with a long tail or brush, widespread in the UK. Foxes of the Scottish Highlands tend to be longer legged and grey-red in colour. They have a varied diet of rabbits, young hares, rats, mice, birds and their eggs, earthworms, beetles, frogs and carrion, with fruit in autumn. 'Frenzy killers' they can invade hen-houses and kill every hen but just eat one.

Red Deer, *Cervus elaphus*, essentially a woodland animal, is the largest wild British land mammal. The Scottish Highlands is its last real stronghold where they largely live on open mountainsides, growing to around 110kg in weight. Although 14 point 'Imperial' stags occur, normally 12 points is the greatest number – a royal stag, with between 20–30 hinds in his harem. In the mating season dominant stags may lose a third of body weight keeping rivals at bay. They live for 15–20 years.

Roe Deer, *Capreolus capreolus*, are delicate, graceful deer with velvety black muzzles. They have no visible tails but a cream-coloured caudal patch instead. Not gregarious, they live in family groups within woodland. They turn tail if they sight a hunter.

Red Squirrel, *Sciuris vulgaris*, are 17cm long russet coloured rodents of which half their size is their bushy tail. They inhabit coniferous forests, especially those containing Norway spruce and Caledonian pine where they feed on pine nuts and cones. Perfectly adapted for climbing trees, they are constantly alert for danger and only venture on to the ground with caution, to recover nuts.

Mountain Hare, *Lepus timidus*, inhabits heather moorland and high grassland in the Scottish Highlands. Smaller and greyer than brown hares, in winter they turn white, camouflaging them above the snowline from predation by golden eagles. Generally they live above ground but may dig holes for protection in cold weather and to shelter their leverets – a doe rearing 4–5 young in spring.

Pipistrelle Bat, *Pipistrellus pipistrellus*, is the smallest of all British bats (with wings folded it can fit inside a matchbox). Once very common it is now in decline. They have dark heads with blackish-brown nose and ears, and black wings, with orange-brown backs and yellow-brown stomachs. They hunt insects uttering high-pitched calls audible to humans. They hibernate less than other bat species.

e Marten

Badger

d Fox

Red Deer

e Deer

Red Squirrel

untain Hare

Pipistrelle Bat

DISCOVER SCOTLAND'S BIRDS
Land Birds

Raptors

Sea Eagle or White-Tailed Sea Eagle, *Haliaetus albicilla*, Scotland's largest raptor has a wingspan up to 2.4m, is up to 85cm tall and 90cm long. Despite their great size they are remarkably agile in flight and easily recognised by their white tail feathers. They inhabit coastal areas and wetlands where their diet is mostly birds and fish.

Golden Eagle, *Aquila chrysaetos*, is widespread in Scotland's mountains. Smaller than the Sea eagle it has a wingspan of up to 2.27m and slightly smaller body. They fly very high, covering a wide area in search of prey which they drop suddenly on to with outspread talons. In late winter and spring they perform elaborate aerial 'cart-wheeling', unusually calling as they display.

Osprey, *Pandion haliaetus*, a Scottish visitor from March to September the Osprey hunts by hovering over lochs before diving at high speeds to hit the water and grasp a fish. Large prey are turned to face forward before taking off again. With a wingspan up to 1.6m and length up to 69cm Ospreys build nests at the top of pine trees to which, annually, they add big sticks.

Hen Harrier, *Circus cyaneus*, are low flying birds when quartering prey. Males are mainly pale grey, whilst females and juveniles have brown plumage and owl-like facial disc. In windy conditions they hold their wings in a 'V' shape, seldom flapping them. With a wingspan of up to 1.20m and length up to 50cm they live and breed in upland moors and bogs and eat small mammals, birds and insects.

Red Kite, *Milvus milvus*, have a distinctively rusty-red body and underwing coverts with pale grey head and wing patches and black wingtips (spanning up to 1.85m) when seen from below. Few birds of prey are more impressive in flight as they are also masters at flying. They eat earthworms, small mammals and carrion.

Peregrine, *Falco peregrinus*, nest on cliffs from which they can spot suitable prey, such as medium-sized birds that they capture by swooping down at speeds of up to 240 kilometres per hour, whereupon small birds can be killed by talon impact alone.

Gamebirds

Capercaillie, *Tetrao urogallus*, is the largest Scottish grouse and it inhabits mature pine and spruce forests. Entirely vegetarian, they feed in the early morning and roost in trees during the day. During courtship in spring males gather at dawn at display areas where they emit very loud clicking and popping calls.

Ptarmigan, *Lagopus mutus*, inhabit Scotland's high mountain tops. They have white wings all year but the camouflaging body plumage changes with the seasons from mottled grey to buff-brown, turning all white in winter. They feed on buds, shoots, berries, and some insects. Gregarious in winter they are territorial during the breeding season.

Red Grouse, *Lagopus lagopus scoticus*, inhabit Scotland's heather moorlands and mountain slopes where they can be seen when flushed from their cover. They have a low gliding flight with rapid bursts of wing beats accompanied by a frantic call.

Black Grouse, *Tetrao tetrix*, prefers marginal forest areas adjacent to bogs and moors where it is a ground feeder. They roost in trees but males display out in the open at dawn. Adult males have a distinctive forked tale. Adult females have mottled brown plumage.

ite-Tailed Sea Eagle

Golden Eagle

prey

Hen Harrier

d Kite

Peregrine

percaillie

Ptarmigan

d Grouse

Black Grouse

Corvids

Chough, *Pyrrhocorax pyrrhocorax*, is found in west Scotland where it inhabits sea cliffs. They feed on a diet principally of ants that they probe from grazed grassland. Masterful fliers they can glide, soar on thermals and perform aerobatics whilst maintaining contact with loud 'cheeow' or 'kiaa' calls.

Raven, *Corvus corax*, are the largest member of the crow family and can be as big as a buzzard. All black in colour with iridescent plumage, most are sedentary and build eyrie-style nests within large foraging areas. In the breeding season they perform spectacular aerial dives and tumbles. They pair for life.

Owls

Short-Eared Owl, This is the most diurnal owl. It nests in young forestry plantations where it is an invaluable predator upon voles that otherwise damage and kill young conifers.

Bunting

Snow Bunting, *Plectrophenax nivalis*, inhabit Scotland's mountain tops where they feed upon seeds and invertebrates. Flocks of snow buntings are sometimes called 'snowflakes' after the 'blizzard' of white feathers when they take off together. Their stance is horizontal and they run rapidly as if by clockwork.

Farm, Garden, and Songbirds

Crested Tit, *Parus cristatus*, is the only European crested small bird. The female nests by excavating a hole in rotten tree stumps, making a new hole each year. Their habitat is mainly pine forest or mixed woodland. They often feed on insects found on tree trunks.

Corncrake, *Crex crex*, is a secretive bird that is very hard to see but easily heard! Summer visitors to Scotland's Western Isles they nest in dense vegetation within hayfields that are harvested late in the season. They fly low and drop quickly into dense cover before running to safety.

Crossbill, *Laxia scotica*, (Scottish Crossbill) is the only bird endemic to Britain. It has a curved crossed bill designed to feed on seeds from Scots pine. Other Crossbills share this adaptation for extracting seeds. In this food choice they have no other bird competitors.

Water Birds
Ducks, Geese and Swans

Eider, *Somateria mollissima*, famed for their nest of downy breast feathers, Eiders are engaging birds to watch when on the water where the black and white male performs crooning and cooing calls whilst throwing their heads back. Having mated the females build a hidden nest ashore where their mottled brown plumage affords excellent camouflage. They feed on bottom dwelling marine organisms, diving to reach them.

Barnacle Goose, *Branta leucopsis*, is a migrant, arriving in October and leaving in March for breeding grounds in Greenland or Spitsbergen. Adults have a white face and black neck, back barred black and grey, under parts white, with black legs and feet. They flock in huge numbers and when they take off in spectacular flights at dawn and dusk.

Whooper Swan, *Cygnus cygnus*, are large, pure white swans, with long necks and a loud trumpeting or bugling call. They over-winter in Scotland and withstand cold well. Family units remain together within large winter flocks.

Mute Swans, *Cygnus olor*, by contrast have shorter necks that they hold in a graceful 'S' shape, and a pointed tail that is raised slightly. In flight their wings beat with a unique humming sound.

ough

Raven

ort-Eared Owl

Snow Bunting

ested Tit

Corncrake

ossbill

Eider

rnacle Geese

Mute Swan

Whooper Swan

Birds of Inland Water

Grey Heron, *Ardea cinerea*, is the most widespread heron in Europe and is frequently seen by Scottish inland and sea lochs standing motionless by the water's edge for hours on end when resting and also fishing with its large dagger-like bill.

Grebe

Great Crested Grebe, *Podiceps cristatus*, are famous for their mating dance when males and females who look alike, raise themselves from the water, breast to breast, feet paddling furiously, and swing their heads from side to side, with brightly coloured head crest raised. Fluffy striped chicks often ride on their parents backs in the water.

Coastal and Seabirds

Shag, *Phalacrocorax aristotelis*, prefers deeper water and rockier coasts than its relative the Cormorant. Adults have an oily green plumage, bottle green eyes, yellow gape and upturned crest. Courtship displays in spring include head and neck rubbing. They make untidy nests, often adorned with seaweed and a variety of flotsam.

Gannet, *Morus bassanus*, Europe's largest breeding sea bird is superbly streamlined and able to plunge-dive from a considerable height, into the sea after herring or mackerel. Black and white in colour with a yellow buff head they fold their wings just before entering the water. In flight they glide, or use deep, powerful wing beats.

Puffin, *Fratercula arctica*, breed in offshore islands and isolated mainland cliffs by burrowing in sloping peaty cliff tops. Colonies are large and may be crowded. Displaying pairs make creaking, growling calls standing bill to bill outside their nests. 'Clown-like' on land, they are expert divers, flyers and underwater swimmers, catching fish and crustaceans.

Fulmar, *Fulmarus glacialis*, nests on sea cliffs where strong updrafts are utilised by the birds in stiff-winged flight as easily as they glide over the waves. They pair for life and greet each other by bobbing and bowing their heads whilst cackling loudly. Large groups often follow trawlers feeding on jettisoned offal.

Guillemot, *Uria aalge*, breeds in large cliff colonies often numbering thousands. Not skilled flyers they often need to make several attempts at landing before they are successful. Better at fishing they often crash through the surface water into shoals spotted from the air. They lay a single, pointed egg, directly on to the cliff ledge.

Gulls

Great Black-Backed Gull, *Larus marinus*, breeds in loose colonies amongst other birds which may become its food source. They scavenge carrion but also hunt seabirds returning to colonies with food which they then steal, or kill the birds themselves. Adults have white heads and bodies, and black wings, but juveniles are banded brown and white with black blotches appearing in their second and third years.

Kittiwake, *Rissa tridactyla*, are found in sheer cliff colonies often with other seabirds. Summer adults are bright white all over with pale yellow bill and brownish-black legs and feet. Juveniles have a blackish zig-zag across grey and white underwing. They have a buoyant flight even in gales and stormy seas.

Shearwater

Manx Shearwater, *Puffinus puffinus*, are best seen from ferries at sea because their habit of returning at night to their nest burrows means that they are difficult to view from land. During the day they fly out at sea in long lines low over the water seeking small fish and squid. They may form groups or 'rafts' that feed together when food is found.

ey Heron

Great Crested Grebe

g

Gannet

fin

Fulmar

llemot

Great Black-Backed Gull

iwake

Manx Shearwater

Skuas

Great Skua, *Stercorarius skua*, is the largest and most aggressive of all skuas. It allows no one near its nest or young, attacking if provoked, showing no fear of any predator. Nesting colonies are near other seabirds for a ready supply of food. Marauders, they attack birds returning with food to make them drop it. Then they catch it before it falls into the sea. In flight these bulky birds look broad-winged and short-tailed.

Waders

Plovers

Dotterel, *Charadrius morinellus*, breeds on remote mountain tops where vegetation is sparse moss and lichen. Males assume nesting responsibility and despite bold markings their sedentary habit makes them hard to spot. The brightly coloured female initiates courtship.

Oystercatcher, *Haematopus ostralegus*, are strikingly black and white birds with bright orange bills. They are common on shorelines rich in cockles and mussels which they feed on, prising apart the valves with their powerful bills. They also probe for marine worms in the mud. Newly fledged juveniles are exceptionally well camouflaged to resemble lichen encrusted rocks.

Greenshank, *Tringa nebularia*, is easily recognised by its long green legs and grey and white plumage, is a scarce breeder in Scotland where it may be seen overwintering on coasts, lake shores and riversides. It is adept at running after small fish which it catches with its slightly upturned bill.

Curlew, *Numenius arquata*, has a long curved bill perfectly adapted for feeding in damp ground on a diet including insects, worms, and molluscs and crustaceans on the sea shore. It has a haunting melodious call in spring when nesting and a 'cour-lee' call year round. Outside the breeding season they normally live in large flocks.

Redshank, *Tringa totanus*, is an inhabitant of wet meadows and coastal marshes in summer: estuaries and shores in winter. It is recognised by its orange-red legs and red base to its bill, mottled grey-brown plumage, white underparts and barred tail. Easily disturbed it gives flight with a ringing alarm call of 'klu-klu-klu'.

Terns

Arctic Tern, *Sterna paradisaea*, is a coastal colonial bird that undergoes the longest migration of any bird and return from Antarctica to their Scottish colonies in May, often sharing them with other sea terns. Aggressively territorial they defend their nests by dive-bombing intruders.

Divers

Black-Throated Diver, *Gavia arctica*, is mostly seen on water where its smooth dives distinguish it from Shags that they can superficially resemble. They are renowned for their territorial displays, where they rush across the water with raised wings before rearing up with neck arched back.

Red-Throated Diver, *Gavia stellata*, is a buoyant swimmer that dives regularly for extended periods. They display during territorial disputes, by gliding across the water surface, calling loudly. Recognised by a dark red throat in summer, this gradually disappears to white for winter.

Great Northern Diver, *Gavia immer*, is a hardy winter visitor perfectly at home on the sea in a gale. They dive almost continuously for crabs and flatfish and like other divers may sometimes roll on to their side to preen all their feathers.

eat Skua

Dotterel

stercatcher

Greenshank

rlew

Redshank

ic Tern

Black-Throated Diver

d-Throated Diver

Great Northern Diver

FISH IN SCOTLAND'S MARINE REALM

Basking Shark – *Cetorhinus maximus*, with characteristic floppy dorsal fin, grows up to 11m long and weighs over 3 tons (3,000kg). A harmless plankton feeder, its gaping mouth and five huge gill slits sieve 1,500 tons (1.5million kg) of water per hour.

Lesser Spotted Dogfish – *Scyliorhinus canicula*, the commonest European shark, is a harmless, bottom feeder of molluscs, crustaceans, and flat-fish. Its sandy brown body has small dark spots, with creamy-white underside. They grow to 100cm in length.

Greater Spotted Dogfish – *Scyliorhinus stellaris*, or Nursehound live over rocky sea-beds and differ from the lesser spotted dogfish by a dorsal fin positioned further forward, and separate nasal flaps. An adult averages 120cm in length.

Porbeagle – *Lamna nasus*, are surface living sharks that hunt mackerel or herring. Deep grey-blue above, pale cream below with a strong keel along each side of the tail and a smaller keel on the tail fin, they grow up to 2.4m. They have three-pointed teeth.

Spotted Ray – *Raja montagui*, has a spotted brown body. Deep water dwellers they reach maturity in nine years with a size of 76cm.

Blonde Ray – *Raja brachyura*, is similar In shape to the spotted ray with dark spots that extend right to the edge of the wings. Blonde rays may reach 110cm long.

Cuckoo Ray – *Raja naevus*, is smaller, at 70cm long, full grown, Cuckoo rays are distinguished by black and yellow 'roundel' markings on the wings.

Thornback Ray – *Raja clavata*, is mottled grey-brown on top, blue-grey underside. Males are spiny all over the upper surface; females have spines only in the front part. Females grow to about 2.7m, males are slightly smaller. It is the commonest ray.

Conger Eel – *Conger conger*, has a smooth skin, no pelvic fins, a slightly protruding lower jaw, a dorsal fin that starts near the head, and large gill slits. A voracious eater it grows to 2.7m. Congers hide in crevices, especially submerged wrecks.

Herring – *Clupea harengus*, have slender grey-green bodies up to 40cm long with delicate, silvery scales, one short dorsal fin and no lateral line. Plankton feeders, they move hundreds of feet vertically in search of food during the course of a day.

Cod – *Gadus morhua*, have three dorsal fins and two ventral fins, and a single barbel under the lower jaw. Darkly mottled on the dorsal surface, they vary from brownish to pale grey according to habitat. They grow to 119cm.

Haddock – *Melanogrammus aeglefinus*, has a small lower jaw with a short chin barbell, and a black blotch between the base of the pectoral fin and lateral line. Its upper body is purplish or greenish-grey with silver sides and white belly. They grow to 76cm.

Poor Cod – *Trisopterus minutus*, with long chin barbel and overlapping upper jaw only growing to 23cm. The back is yellowish, the underside silvery-grey, with a small black spot on the upper part of the pectoral fin base.

Saithe, Coley, or Coalfish – *Pollachius virens*, belongs to the Cod family. With equal length jaws, straight pale lateral line, and dark green fins. They grow up to 60cm.

Whiting – *Merlangius merlangus*, is slender and grows to 45cm, or exceptionally 70cm. Sandy-green on the back with silver sides, a distinctive black spot is situated at the base of the pectoral fin. They have a shorter lower jaw and no barbel.

asse

Ray

npsucker

Cod

king Shark

Plaice

ttish Salmon

Conger Eel

Ling – *Molva molva*, is an elongate, slim fish, ling with a single long barbel on the lower jaw, a greenish-brown marbled body, with elongated, white-tipped second dorsal and anal fins. A dark spot marks the hind edge of the first dorsal fin. They grow to 200cm.

Angler Fish – *Lophius piscatorius*, is a bottom-dweller varying from reddish-brown to grey-green above, with white below. The large head is surmounted by a lure formed from spines of the first dorsal ray. They may grow up to 1.8m long.

Red and Grey Gurnards – *Trigla spp* has a distinctly red or pink upper body with orange or white underside, an armoured head, and large pectoral fins used for walking. Bottom feeders, they grow up to 77cm. Grey are more common than red gurnards.

Mackerel – *Scomber scombrus*, have slender crescent-shaped fins, iridescent blue-green stripes with white undersurfaces. Additional to two dorsal fins are 4–6 finlets, more finlets lie between the ventral fin and tail. They grow to 40cm, rarely 66cm.

Red Band-fish – *Cepola rubescens*, this large eyed, slender bodied fish has a red or orange body with a long dorsal fin. They may grow up to 70cm long.

Cuckoo Wrasse – *Labrus mixtus*, have reddish-orange females with three dark blotches along the back, and males with brilliant blue heads with blue streaked sides on a yellow or orange colour. Spawning males have a white head patch. They grow to 33cm.

Ballan Wrasse – *Labrus bergylta*, are born female, become sexually mature at six years and after several spawning seasons may become male. Deep bodied with small mouths adapted for crushing molluscs and crustaceans, they vary from green-brown to red-brown, or chestnut. The scales appear spotted. They reach 60cm in length.

Lesser Sand Eel – *Ammodytes tobianus*, is not a true eel but has an eel-like shape for swimming, and burrowing in the sand. Its shiny body is tinged yellow with a silver belly. The lower jaw protrudes on the pointed snout. They grow to a maximum of 15cm.

Turbot – *Scophthalmus maximus*, closely match their background being sandy-brown with small darker brown speckles. Their flat body is almost circular, the eyed side being covered in scattered bony tubercles, not scales. They grow up to 100cm.

Plaice – *Pleuronectes platessa*, has smooth brown skin with bright orange or red spots on the eyed side and white beneath. Between 4 and 7 bony knobs run in a curved line from behind the eyes to the beginning of the slightly arched lateral line. Usually about 50cm, plaice can live up to 20 years and grow up to 90cm and weigh as much as 8lb (3.6kg).

Lumpsucker *Cyclopterus lumpus* spawns March to May, the orange male devotedly guarding 200,000 eggs rarely leaving them even to eat. Defending against predators he fans the eggs constantly to aerate them. Females are blue-green and can grow to 60cm.

Halibut – *Hippoglossus hippoglossus*, are mottled sandy-brown with a large mouth, strongly arched lateral line and pointed strong teeth. Voracious predators of fish and large crustaceans, they are the largest of the flatfish and grow up to 250cm.

Salmon – *Salmo salar*, are silver in colour and slightly plump from a diet of small herrings, sand eels and crustaceans. Salmon undergo strenuous journeys to spawn in fresh water when they swim through rapids and leap waterfalls. Large salmon can leap heights of 3m.

DISCOVER SCOTLAND'S ROCK POOLS

'A world within a world' rock pools are found at all levels on unpolluted rocky shores in Scotland. They are localised areas where the eroded coastal rock platform, has basins of different shapes, sizes, and depths, with widely different volumes of water. Rock pools never dry out and are the most beautiful and rewarding environments on the seashore, containing organisms sensitive to desiccation or that cannot tolerate drying effects at all.

Each rock pool has its own, unique, physical characteristics, and its organisms may need special physiological adaptations to cope with the widely fluctuating changes in temperature, salinity and pH that can occur. A pool high on a rocky shore, exposed to sunlight and or rain for a fortnight, then inundated by a high spring tide, is subject to extremes that a rock pool low on the shore does not experience for such lengths of time. So these pools are generally species poor. Rock pools on the low and middle range shore, which experience regular tidal changes, by contrast, contain a rich and varied selection of shore organisms.

When investigating a rock pool care must be taken not to disturb the water unduly when parting seaweed as this may drive prawns and fish, active swimmers, into hiding places in cracks and crevices, whilst tubeworms and anemones will withdraw their fans or tentacles. All will gradually re-emerge if the water is left undisturbed. Sea urchins, starfish, crabs, marine snails and bivalves, as well as nudibranch (shell-less) molluscs can all be found, together with sponges and hydrozoans.

Upper shore rock pools are characterised by green seaweeds such as, gaseous, *Enteromorpha intestinalis* that float amongst their bubbles, often in quite small rock pools. Around the rocky edges the green woodlouse-like crustacean *Ligia oceanica*, or sea slater, may be found hiding in crevices together with the tiny serrated shelled winkle *Littorina neritoides*.

Middle shore rock pools may contain the encrusting pink alga *Lithothamnion*, whilst the coralline red alga, *Corallina officianalis* forms tree-like forests in which tiny hydroids grow and amongst which shrimps and small gastropods shelter. Flat-shelled limpets, lacking the conical domes of their exposed relatives, create home bases on the rocky surface alongside edible winkles *Littorina littorea*, crimson beadlet anemones *Actinia equina* and pinky-green Dahlia anemones *Tealia felina*. The shore crab *Carcinus meanus* may scuttle out from a covering of the brown seaweed *Fucus serratus*, under which may be the flattened, spiny, circular shell of the tiny sea urchin *Psammechinus miliaris*. Hermit crabs, *Eupagurus bernhardus*, scurry across the pool floor seeking out new homes from a scattering of empty winkle shells. Prawns trapped by the falling tide rapidly back-swim if they sense a disturbance. *Nucella lapillus*, the common dog whelk, a carnivorous snail glides around looking mussels to prey upon.

Lower shore rock pools just above low water contain the leathery brown fronds of the kelp seaweed *Laminaria digitata* and the crinkled fronds of *Laminaria saccharina*, both colonized by microscopic hydroids, encrusting sponges, sea slugs and sea hares – retiring, prettily coloured soft bodied molluscs, with internal shells. Dark rocky overhangs are often encrusted with plant-like animals, including hydroids, sponges, sea mats, anemones, tubeworms and sea squirts, together with sea slugs, snails and the worms that feed on them. **LOOK, PHOTOGRAPH, – BUT DON'T COLLECT.**

MAMMALS AND BIRDS YOU COULD DISCOVER

In the West Highlands and Islands, Loch Lomond, Stirling and The Trossachs

Mammals: Bottlenose dolphin, Common seal, Common dolphin, Grey seal, Fallow deer, Minke whale, Mountain hare, Natterer bat, Otter, Porpoise, Pipistrelle bat, Pine marten, Rabbit, Red deer, Red squirrel, Roe deer, Weasel, Wild feral goats.

Birds: Barn owl, Barnacle goose, Black grouse, Blue tit, Buzzard, Chough, Cormorant, Corncrake, Curlew, Divers, Fulmar, Gannet, Golden eagle, Golden eye, Greylag goose, Guillemot, Hen harrier, Heron, Kittiwake, Lapwing, Merlin, Mute swan, Osprey, Oystercatcher, Puffin, Razorbill, Raven, Razorbill, Red grouse, Red kite, Redshank, Redstart, Sand martin, Sea eagle or White-tailed sea eagle, Sedge warbler, Shag, Shearwater, Skua, Sparrow Hawk, Spotted flycatcher, Snipe, Snow bunting, Tern, Tree pipit, Tufted duck, Twite, Waders, Whooper swan, Whinchat, Wigeon, Woodcock.

Reptiles: Adder, Common lizard.

Fish: Basking shark.

Insects: Demoiselle dragonfly, March fritillary butterfly, Narrow bordered bee halk-moth, Scotch Argus butterfly, Speckled wood butterfly.

In the Outer Hebrides

Mammals: Bottlenose dolphin, Common dolphin, Grey seal, Orca, Otter, Porpoise, Soay sheep.

Birds: Auk, Black-throated diver, Black guillemot, Corncrake, Corn bunting, Fulmar, Herring gull, Gannet, Greenshank, Guillemot, Kittiwake, Leach's petrel, Puffin, Razorbill, Sea eagle, Storm petrel, Tern, Waders,

Others: Crab, Lobsters.

Insects: Great Yellow bumblebee.

MAMMALS AND BIRDS YOU COULD DISCOVER

In the Northern Isles

Mammals: Bottlenose dolphin, Common seal, Common dolphin, Grey seal, Mountain hare, Orca, Otter, Porpoise.

Birds: Arctic tern, Arctic skua, Auks, Black guillemot, Curlew, Dunlin, Eider duck, Fulmar, Gannet, Golden plover, Great skua, Guillemot, Hen harrier, Kittiwake, Lapwing, Mallard, Merlin, Purple sandpiper, Puffin, Oystercatcher, Razorbill, Red grouse, Red-necked phalarope, Redshank, Red-throated diver, Ringed plover, Shag, Short-eared owl, Shoveler, Snipe, Storm petrel, Teal, Turnstone, Waders, Whimbrel, Wigeon,

Insects: Emperor moth, dragonflies,

Sea shore invertebrates: Anemones, Dead man's fingers, crabs, jellyfish, sunstars, urchins,

In South and Central Scotland

Mammals: Porpoise, Common seal, Grey seal, Red deer, Roe deer, Sika deer, Otter, Badger, Red fox, Water vole, Mountain hare, Rabbit, Red squirrel, Pipistrelle bat, Weasel, Wild goat.

Birds: Barn owl, Barnacle goose, Blackcap, Black grouse, Blue tit, Buzzard, Coal tit, Cormorant, Crested grebe, Crossbill, Curlew, Dipper, Eider, Fulmar, Garden warbler, Gannet, Golden eagle, Goosander, Great spotted woodpecker, Green woodpecker, Grey wagtail, Guillemot, Hen Harrier, Heron, Jay, Kestrel, Kingfisher, Kittiwake, Little grebe, Lapwing, Mallard, Moorhen, Mute swan, Nuthatch, Osprey, Oystercatcher, Peregrine, Pied flycatcher, Pintail, Puffin, Razorbill, Raven, Red grouse, Redshank, Redstart, Reed bunting, Sedge warbler, Shag, Short-eared owl, Siskin, Sparrowhawk, Snipe, Stonechat, Swallow, Tawny owl, Teal, Tern, Tufted duck, Twite, Waders, Water Fowl, Water rail, Wheatear, Whooper swan, Whitethroat, Wigeon, Willow Warbler, Woodcock, Wood Warbler, Wren.

Reptiles: Adder, Common lizard.

Amphibia: Great crested newt, frog, Natterjack toad.

Insects: Dragonfly, Damselfly, Large heath butterfly, Scotch Argus butterfly.

MAMMALS AND BIRDS YOU COULD DISCOVER

In Perthshire, Angus & Dundee and the Kingdom of Fife

Mammals: Bottlenose dolphin, Badger, Grey seal, Fallow deer, Mountain hare, Otter, Pine marten, Red deer, Red squirrel, Roe deer, Sika deer, Whales, Wildcat, Wild feral goat.

Birds: Black-necked grebe, Black-tailed godwit, Buzzard, Capercaillie, Coot, Crossbill, Divers, Dunlin, Eider duck, Falcons, Gadwall, Gannet, Golden eagle, Golden eye, Great crested grebe, Greylag goose, Grouse, Guillemot, Heron, Kestrel, Kittiwake, Knot, Lapwing, Long-tailed duck, Mallard, Mute swan, Osprey, Oystercatcher, Pink-footed goose, Pintail, Pochard, Ptarmigan, Puffin, Raven, Razorbill, Red grouse, Redpoll, Redshank, Redstart, Red-throated diver, Ring ouzel, Scoter, Sea duck, Sedge warbler, Shag, Shearwater, Shelduck, Shoveler, Snipe, Spotted redshank, Stonechat, Teal, Tern, Tits, Tree pipit, Tufted duck, Turnstone, Whooper swan, Wigeon, Willow warbler.

Butterflies: Common blue, Meadow brown, Orange-tip, Painted lady, Peacock, Red admiral, Ringlet, and Small copper.

In Aberdeen and Grampian Highlands

Mammals: Badger, Bats, Bottlenose dolphin Common seal, Grey seal, Fox, Highland cattle, Minke whale, Mountain hare, Otter, Red deer, Roe deer, Red squirrel.

Birds: Arctic tern, Bittern, Black grouse, Black guillemot, Buzzard, Capercaillie, Common tern, Cormorant, Crested tit, Crossbill, Eider duck, Fulmar, Gannet, Geese, Green woodpecker, Golden eagle, Golden eye, Grouse, Guillemot, Herring gull, Kittiwake, Lapwing, Mute swan, Osprey, Peregrine, Pink-footed goose, Porpoise, Puffin, Razorbill, Redshank, Red-throated diver, Reed bunting, Shag, Siskin, Snow bunting, Stonechat, Teal, Waders, Whooper swan, Wigeon, Wintering wildfowl, Woodland birds.

In the Highlands

Mammals: Badger, bats, Common seal, Bottlenose dolphin, Grey seal, Mountain hare, Otter, Porpoise, Pine marten, Puffin, Red deer, Red squirrel, Roe deer, Sika deer, Whales, Wildcat.

Birds: Arctic skua, Barnacle goose, Bar-tailed godwit, Black grouse, Black-throated diver, Buzzard, Capercaillie, Common sandpiper, Cormorant, Crested tit, Crossbill, Curlew, Dipper, Dotterel, Dunlin, Eider duck, Hen harrier, Heron, Fulmar, Gannet, Golden eagle, Golden eye, Golden plover, Great northern diver, Great skua, Greenfinch, Greenshank, Greylag goose, Guillemot, Kestrel, Kittiwake, Lapwing, Little grebe, Mallard, Manx shearwater, Merlin, Merganser, Osprey, Oystercatcher, Peregrine, Plovers, Ptarmigan, Puffin, Raven, Razorbill, Red grouse, Red kite, Red poll, Redshank, Redstart, Red-throated diver, Ring ouzel, Sandpiper, Sea eagle, Shag, Shelduck, Slavonian grebe, Snipe, Sparrowhawk, Spotted flycatcher, Stonechat, Tawny owl, Twite, Wheatear, Whooper swan, Whinchat, Wigeon, Willow warbler, Woodcock, Woodwarbler.

DISCOVER SCOTLAND'S WILDLIFE

Places to visit, tours to enjoy, discovering Scotland's wildlife

South of Scotland
– Dumfries & Galloway, Ayrshire & Arran, and Scottish Borders.

1. **FCS – Arran Forests.**
   South Arran. Tel 01770 302218
   www.forestry.gov.uk/scotland

2. **SNH – Caerlaverock National Nature Reserve.**
   Dumfries. Tel 01387 770275

3. **WWT – Caerlaverock Wetlands Centre.**
   Dumfries. Tel 01387 770275

4. **SNH – Cairnsmore of Fleet.**
   Tel 01557 814435

5. **SWT – Carstramon Wood.**
   Tel 0131 312 7765

6. **Clifftop Discovery Ltd.**
   Tel 018907 71838
   www.clifftopdiscovery.co.uk

7. **Cream o' Galloway.**
   Tel 01557 814040
   www.creamogalloway.co.uk

8. **NTS – Culzean Country Park.**
   12 miles south of Ayr.
   Tel 0844 493 2149

9. **Cumbrae Voyages.**
   Largs, Tel 0845 257040
   www.cumbraevoyages.co.uk

10. **FCS – Dalbeattie Forest.**
    Tel 01387 247745
    www.forestry.gov.uk/scotland

11. **RBGE – Dawyck Botanic Garden.**
    Peeblesshire, Tel 01721 760254
    www.rbge.org.uk

12. **Drumlanrig Castle Gardens and Country Park.**
    Tel 01848 331555
    www.drumlanrig.com

13. **Visit Dumfries and Galloway.**
    Tel 01387 253862
    www.visitdumfriesandgalloway.co.uk

14. **FCS – Earshaig Forest.**
    Nr Beattock, Tel 01387 860247
    www.forestry.gov.uk/scotland

15. **FCS – Galloway Forest Park.**
    Tel 01671 402165
    www.forestry.gov.uk/gallowayforestpark
    Email Galloway@forestry.gsi.gov.uk

16. **FCS – Galloway Red Deer Range.**
    Tel 01671 402420
    www.forestry.gov.uk/gallowayforestpark
    Email Galloway@forestry.gsi.gov.uk

17. **Glenholm Wildlife Project.**
    Broughton, Tel 01899 830408
    www.glenholmwildlife.co.uk

18. **FCS – Glentress & Kailzie Gardens Tweed Valley Osprey Project.**
    Tel 0845 367 3787
    www.forestry.gov.uk/tweedvalleyospreys
    Email sarah.oakley@forestry.gsi.goc.uk

19. **NTS – Grey Mare's Tail.**
    Moffat, Tel 01556 502575

20. **Kippford Park.**
    Nr Dalbeatie, Tel 01556 62063
    www.kippfordholidaypark.co.uk

21. **SNH – Kirkconnell Flow.**
    Dumfries, Tel 01387 247010

22. **Kirkwood Cottages.**
    Lockerbie, Tel 01576 51020
    www.kirkwood-lockerbie.co.uk

23. **SWT – Knockshinnoch Lagoons.**
    New Cumnock, Tel 0131 312 7765

24. **SWT – Knowetop Lochs.**
    Nr Corsock, D&G,
    Tel 0131 312 7765

25. **RBGE – Logan Botanic Garden.**
    Stranraer, Tel 01776 860231

26. **FCS – Mabie Forest.**
    Dumfries, Tel 01387 860247
    www.forestry.gov.uk/scotland

27. **Mersehead.**
    Dumfries. Tel 01387 780579

28. **Mull of Galloway.**
    Drummore, Tel 01776 840539

29. **Paxton House and Country Park.**
    Berwick on Tweed,
    Tel 01289 386291
    www.paxtonhouse.com

30. **SWT – Pease Dean.**
    Pease Bay, Tel 0131 312 7765

31. **Philiphaugh Estate.**
    Nr Selkirk, Tel 01750 21766
    www.salmonviewingcentre.com

32. **Press Mains Cottages.**
    Coldingham, Tel 01890 771310
    www.pressmainscottages.co.uk

33. **FCS – Red Kite Trail in Dumfries and Galloway.**
    Castle Douglas, Tel 01671 402420
    www.gallowaykitetrail.com

34. **Scottish Seabird Centre.**
    North Berwick, Tel 01620 890202
    www.seabird.org

35. **St Abb's Head.**
    Coldingham, Tel 01890 771443

36. **Threave Garden and Estate.**
    Castle Douglas, Tel 01556 502575

37. **FCS – Tweed Valley Forest Park, Osprey Project.**
    Peebles-Selkirk, Tel 01750 721120
    www.forestry.gov.uk/scottishborders
    www.kailziegardens.com

38. **Wood of Cree,**
    Newton Stewart, Tel 01671 402861

Central Belt of Scotland
– Edinburgh & Lothians, Greater Glasgow & Clyde Valley.

1. **Beecraigs Country Park.**
   Linlithgow, Tel 01506 844516
   www.beecraigs.com

2. **SWT – Carlingnose Point.**
   North Queensferry,
   Tel 0131 312 7765

3. **Clyde Muirshiel Regional Park.**
   Lochwinnoch, Tel 01505 842803
   www.clydemuirshiel.co.uk

4. **SWT – Cumbernauld Glen.**
   Cumbernauld, Tel 0131 312 7765

5. **Dalkeith Country Park.**
   Midlothian, Tel 0131 654 1666
   www.dalkeithcountrypark.co.uk

6. **SWT – Erraid Wood,**
   Hillend, Edinburgh,
   Tel 0131 312 7765

7. **SWT – Falls of Clyde.**
   New Lanark, Tel 01555 665262

8. **Lochwinnoch.**
   Renfrewshire, Tel 01505 842663

9. **SWT – Lower Nethan Gorge.**
   Crossford, Tel 0131 312 7765

10. **Maid of the Forth.**
    South Queensferry,
    Tel 0131 331 4857
    www.maidoftheforth.co.uk

11. **SWT – Possil Marsh**.
High Possil, Tel 0131 312 7765

12. **SWT – Red Moss of Balerno**.
Balerno, Tel 0131 312 7765

13. **RBGE – Royal Botanic Garden**.
Edinburgh, Tel 0131 552 7171

14. **Strathclyde Country Park**.
Motherwell. Tel 01698 402060
www.northian.gov.uk

15. **Water of Leith Visitor Centre**.
Edinburgh, Tel 0131 455 7367
www.waterofleith.org.uk

West Highland & Islands, Loch Lomond, Stirling & Trossachs.

1. **About Argyll Walking Holidays**.
Tel 01369 860272
www.aboutargyll.co.uk

2. **About Mull**.
Bunessan, Mull,
Tel 01681 700 507
www.aboutmull.co.uk

3. **Alternative Boat Hire**.
Tel 01681 700537
www.boatripsiona.com

4. **Argaty Red Kites**.
Doune, Tel 01786 841373
www.argatyredkites.co.uk

5. **FCS – Argyll Forest Park**.
Arrochar, Tel 01301 702432
www.forestry.gov.uk/argyllforestpark

6. **FCS – Aros Park & Loch Frisa**.
Mull, Tel 01680 300640
www.forestry.gov.uk/scotland
Email jan.dunlop@forestry.gsi.gov.uk

7. **FCS – Barnaline**.
Lochgilphead, Tel 01546 602518
www.forestry.gov.uk/scotland

8. **RGBE – Benmore Botanic Garden**.
Dunoon, Tel 01369 706261

9. **Isle of Coll**.
Tel 01879 230301

10. **Craignish Cruises**.
Ardfern, Tel 01852 500540
Mob 0774 702038
www.criagnishcruises.co.uk

11. **FCS – David Marshall Lodge Visitor Centre**.
Aberfoyle, Tel 01877 382258
www.forestry.gov.uk/qefp

12. **Discover Mull**.
Isle of Mull, Tel 01688 400415
Mob 07780 600367
www.discovermull.co.uk

13. **Farsain Cruises**.
Craobh Haven, Tel 01852 500664

14. **Firth of Lorn Cruises**,
Isle of Colonsay, Tel 01951 200320
www.colonsay.org.uk

15. **Gartmore Dam Country Park**,
Clackmannanshire,
Tel 01259 214319
www.clacksweb.org.uk

16. **Gemini Cruises**.
Crinan, Tel 01546 830208
www.gemini-crinan.co.uk

17. **SNH. Glasdrum Wood**.
Loch Creran, Tel 01546 603611

18. **FCS. Glen Nant NNR**.
Taynuilt, Tel 01631 566155
www.forestry.gov.uk/scotland
Email lorne.district@forestry.gsi.gov.uk

19. **Hebridean Adventure Centre**.
Tobermory, Mull,
Tel 01688 302044

20. **Hebridean Whale and Dolphin Trust**.
Tobermory, Mull, Tel 01688 302262
www.hwdt.org

21. **Inversnaid**.
Loch Lomond, Tel 0141 331 0993

22. **Islay Birding**.
Isle of Islay, Tel 01496 850010
www.islaybirding.co.uk

23. **Islay Marine Charters**.
Isle of Islay, Tel 01496 850436
www.islaymarine.co.uk

24. **Islay Stalking**.
Isle of Islay, Tel 01496 850120
www.thegearach.co.uk

25. **Islay Wildlife Information Centre**.
Isle of Islay, Tel 01496 850288
www.islaywildlife.freeserve.co.uk

26. **Isle of Jura Exploration**.
Isle of Jura, Tel 07899 912116

27. **FCS – Knapdale Forest**.
Lochgilphead, Tel 01546 602518

28. **SWT – Loch Ardinning**.
Strathblane, Tel 0131 312 7765
www.forestry.gov.uk/scotland

29. **Loch Etive Cruises**.
Taynuilt, Tel 01866 822430
www.oban.org.uk

30. **FCS – Loch Frisa**.
Isle of Mull, Tel 01631 566155

31. **Loch Gruinart**.
Isle of Islay, Tel 01496 850505

32. **SNH – Loch Lomond**.
Balmaha, Tel 01360 870470

33. **SNH – Moine Mhor**.
Kilmartin, Tel 01546 603611

34. **Isle of Mull Encounter Wildlife & Birdwatch Safaris**.
Tel 01680 300441
www.mullwildlife.co.uk

35. **Isle of Mull Wildlife Expeditions**.
Tel 01688 500121
www.scotlandwildlife.com

36. **The Oa**,
Port Ellen, Isle of Islay,
Tel 01496 8505051

37. **FCS – Queen Elizabeth Forest Park**.
Aberfoyle, Tel 01877 382258
www.forestry.gov.uk/qefp
cowal.trossachs.fd@forestry.gsi.gov.uk

38. **Scottish Sea Life Sanctuary**.
Oban, Tel 01631 720386
www.sealsanctuary.co.uk

39. **Sea.fari Adventures**.
Oban, Tel 01852 300003
www.seafari.co.uk

40. **Sealife Adventures**.
Oban, Tel 01852 300203
www.sealife-adventures.com

41. **Sea Life Surveys**.
Isle of Mull, Tel 01688 302916
www.sealifesurveys.com

42. **SWT – Shian Wood**.
Loch Creran, Tel 0131 312 7765

43. **NTS – Staffa**.
by Isle of Mull, Tel 01463 232034

44. **FCS – Tarbert and Skipness Forest**.
Lochgilphead, Tel 01546 602518
www.forestry.gov.uk/scotland

45. **SNH – Taynish**.
Tayvallich, Tel 01546 603611

46. **Turus Mara**.
Isle of Mull, Tel 01688 400242
www.turusmara.com

47. **Yacht Corrievreckan**.
Kilmore, Oban, Tel 01631 770246
www.corryvreckan.co.uk

Perthshire, Angus & Dundee, and the Kingdom of Fife.

1. **Anstruther Pleasure Trips**.
Anstruther, Tel 01333 310103
www.isleofmayferry.com

2. **Atholl Estates**.
(Ranger Service), Blair Atholl,
Tel 01796 481355
www.athollestatesrangerservice.co.uk

3. **SWT – Bankhead Moss**.
Cupar, Tel 0131 312 7765

4. **Ben Lawers**.
Killin, Tel 01567 820397

5. **SNH – Corrie Fee**.
Glenshee, Tel 01575 550233

6. **SWT – Culaloe**.
Aberdour, Tel 0131 312 7765

7. **SWT – Dumbarnie Links.**
   Leven, Tel 0131 312 7765
8. **SWT – Fleecefaulds Meadow.**
   Cupar, Tel 0131 312 7765
9. **Highland Adventure Safaris.**
   Aberfeldy, Tel 01887 820071
   www.highlandadventuresafaris.co.uk
10. **SNH – Isle of May.**
    Anstruther, Tel 01334 654038
11. **NTS – Killiecrankie.**
    Pitlochry, Tel 01796 473233
12. **SWT – Kilminning Coast.**
    Crail, Tel 0131 312 7765
13. **SNH – Loch Leven.**
    Kinross, Tel 01577 864439
14. **Loch of Kinnordy.**
    Kirriemuir, Tel 01738 630783
15. **SWT – Loch of Lintrathen.**
    Bridgend of Lintrathen,
    Tel 0131 312 7765
16. **SWT – Loch of the Lowes.**
    Dunkeld, Tel 01350 727337
17. **SWT – Montrose Basin.**
    Montrose, Tel 01674 676336
18. **Perthshire – Big Tree Country.**
    Perth, Tel 01738 450600
    www.perthshire.co.uk
19. **FCS – Queen's View
    Visitor Centre.**
    Garry Bridge, Tel 01350 727284
    www.forestry.gov.uk/tayforestpark
20. **The Scottish Deer Centre.**
    Cupar, Tel 01337 810391
21. **FCS – Tay Forest Park.**
    Tel 01350 727284
    www.forestry.gov.uk/tayforestpark
22. **FCS – Tentsmuir.**
    Tayport, Tel 01382 553704
    www.forestry.gov.uk/scotland
23. **RSPB – Vane Farm.**
    Loch Leven, Tel 01577 862355
24. **Wild Perthshire.**
    Dunkeld, Tel 0844 848 4455
    www.wildperthshire.com
25. **Wild Outdoors.**
    Ladybank, Fife,
    Tel 01377 831 196
    www.wildoutdoors.info

Aberdeen and Grampian Highlands.

1. **Balmoral Estate Luxury
   Land Rover Safaris.**
   Balmoral, Tel 01339 742534
   www.balmoralcastle.com
2. **Balmoral Estate Ranger
   Service, Balmoral.**
   Tel 013397 4253
   www.balmoralcastle.com

3. **FCS – Bennachie.**
   Inverurie, Tel 01466 794161
   www.forestry.gov.uk/scotland
4. **FCS – Blackhall Forest.**
   Banchory, Tel 01330 844537
   www.forestry.gov.uk/blackhallforest
5. **FCS – Cambus O'May Forest.**
   Ballater, Tel 01330 844537
   www.forestry.gov.uk/cambusomay
6. **FCS – Culbin & Roseisle.**
   Nr Forres, Tel 01343 820223
   www.forestry.gov.uk/scotland
7. **SNH – Forvie.**
   Aberdeen, Tel 01358 751330
8. **Fowlsheugh.**
   Stonehaven, Tel 01224 624824
9. **Gemini Explorer.**
   Burghead, Morayshire,
   Tel 07747 626280
   www.geminiexplorer.co.uk
10. **SWT – Gight Wood.**
    Methlick, Tel 0131 312 7765
11. **SNH – Glen Tanar National
    Nature Reserve.**
    Aboyne, Tel 01224 642863
12. **Glen Tanar Estate.**
    Aboyne, Tel 013398 86451
    www.glentanar.co.uk
13. **Glenlivet Estate.**
    Tomintoul, Tel 01807 580283
    www.glenlivetestate.co.uk
14. **Glenlivet Wildlife.**
    Ballindalloch, Tel 01807 590 241
    www.glenlivet-wildlife.co.uk
15. **FCS – Huntly Peregrine
    Wildwatch.**
    Huntly, Tel 01466 794161
    www.forestry.gov.uk/peregrines
16. **RSPB – Loch of Strathbeg.**
    Nr Crimond, Tel 01346 532017
17. **MacDuff Marine Aquarium.**
    MacDuff, Tel 01261 833369
    www.marine-aquarium.com
18. **Mar Lodge Estate.**
    Braemar, Tel 013397 41433
19. **Moray Diving.**
    Findhorn, Tel 01309 690421
    www.moraydiving.com
20. **NORTH 58 Sea Adventures.**
    Banff, Tel 07854 447720
    www.north58.co.uk
21. **Puffin Cruises.**
    MacDuff, Tel 01261 832425
    www.puffincruises.com
22. **SNH – St Cyrus.**
    Montrose, Tel 01674 830736
23. **SWT – Spey Bay.**
    Elgin, Tel 0131 312 7765
24. **WalkDeeside Ltd.**
    Aboyne, Tel 01339 880081
    www.walkdeeside.com

The Highlands of Scotland.

1. **Activities Outdoors.**
   Kilchoan, Tel 01972 510212
2. **Applecross Trust.**
   Inverness, Tel 01463 715961
   www.applecrosstrust.org.uk
3. **Ardnamurchan Natural
   History Centre.**
   Acharacle, Tel 01972 500209
   www.arnamurchannaturalhistorycentre.co.uk
4. **Arisaig Marine Ltd.**
   Arisaig, Tel 01687 450224
   www.arisaig.co.uk
5. **SNH – Ariundle Oakwood.**
   Strontian, Tel 01397 704716
6. **Aros, Portree.**
   Isle of Skye, Tel 01478 613649
   www.aros.co.uk
7. **SNH – Beinn Eighe.**
   Kinlochewe, Tel 01445 760254
8. **Bella Jane Boat Trips.**
   Elgol, Isle of Skye,
   Tel 0800 731 3089
   www.bellajane.co.uk
9. **SWT – Ben Mor Coigach.**
   Achiltibuie, Tel 0131 312 7765
10. **SNH – Ben Wyvis.**
    Nr Inverness, Tel 01349 865333
11. **Boots 'N' Paddles.**
    Kirkhill, Tel 0845612 5567
    www.bootsnpaddles.com
12. **Caledonian Discovery Ltd.**
    Fort William, Tel 01397 772167
    www.fingal-cruising.co.uk
13. **Claish Moss.**
    Loch Shiel, Tel 01397 704716
    www.nnr-scotland.org.uk
14. **RSPB – Corrimony.**
    Nr Inverness, Tel 01463 715000
15. **SNH – Craigellachie.**
    Nr Inverness, Tel 01479 810477
16. **Crannog Cruises.**
    Fort William, Tel 01397 700714
    www.crannog.net
17. **SNH – Creag Meagaidh**
    Nr Laggan, Tel 01528 544265
18. **The Dolphin and Seal Centre,**
    North Kessock, Tel 01463 731866
19. **Dolphin Trips – Avoch Ltd,**
    Avoch, Tel 01381 622383
    www.dolphintripsavoch.co.uk
20. **Dunnet Head
    Educational Trust.**
    Thurso, Tel 01847 851991
    www.dunnethead.com
21. **Eco Ventures.**
    Cromarty, Tel 01381 600323
    www.ecoventures.co.uk
22. **SWT – Isle of Eigg.**
    Tel 0131 312 7765

23. Family's Pride II Glassbottom Boat Trips.
Isle of Skye,
www.glassbottomboat.co.uk

24. FCS – Ferry Wood.
Lairg, Tel 01862 810359
www.forestry.gov.uk/scotland

25. Forsinard.
Nr Helmsdale, Tel 01641 571225

26. Gairloch Marine Life Centre and Cruises.
Gairloch, Tel 01445 712636
www.porpoise-gairloch.co.uk

27. FCS – Garbh Eilean All-Abilities Wildlife Hide.
Fort William, Tel 01397 702184
www.forestry.gov.uk/scotland

28. FCS – Glen Affric.
Cannich, Tel 01320 366322
www.forestry.gov.uk/scotland

29. FCS – Glen Brittle.
Skye, c/o Fort Augustus,
Tel 01320 366322
www.forestry.gov.uk/scotland

30. SNH – Glen Roy.
Fort William, Tel 01397 704716

31. Glenloy Wildlife.
Banavie, Fort William,
Tel 01397 712700

32. Glenborrodale.
Loch Sunart, Tel 01463 715000

33. SNH – Glencripesdale.
Loch Sunart, Tel 01397 704716

34. FCS – Glenmore Forest Park.
Glenmore, Strathspey,
Tel 01479 861220
www.forestry.gov.uk/glenmoreforestpark

35. FCS – Great Glen Forest.
between Fort William/Inverness,
Tel 01320 366322
www.forestry.gov.uk/scotland

36. SWT – Handa Island.
Nr Tarbet, Tel 0131 312 7765

37. Heatherlea (Scotland) Ltd.
Nethybridge, Tel 01479 821248
www.heatherlea.co.uk

38. Highland Wildlife and Birdwatch Safaris.
Aviemore, Tel 01479 811169
www.highlandwildlifesafaris.co.uk

39. Highland Wildlife Park.
Kingussie, Tel 01540 651270
www.highlandwildlifepark.org

40. SNH – Inchnadamph.
Nr Ullapool, Tel 01854 613418

41. RSPB – Insh Marshes.
Kingussie, Tel 01540 661518

42. International Otter Survival Fund (IOSF).
Broadford, Isle of Skye,
Tel 01471 822487
www.otter.org

43. NTS – Inverewe Garden.
Gairloch, Tel 01445 781200

44. John o'Groats Ferries.
Caithness, Tel 01955 611353
www.jogferry.co.uk

45. Knockan Crag.
Ullapool, Tel 01854 613418
www.knockan-crag.co.uk

46. FCS – Kylerhea Otter Haven.
Isle of Skye, Tel 01320 366322
www.forestry.gov.uk/scotland

47. Landmark Forest Theme Park.
Carrbridge, Tel 01479 841613
www.landmark-center.co.uk

48. SNH – Loch a' Mhuilinn.
Scourie, Tel 01854 613418

49. SNH – Loch Fleet.
Nr Golspie, Tel 0131 312 7765

50. RSPB – Loch Garten Osprey Centre Abernethy Forest Nature Reserve.
Aviemore, Tel 01479 821409

51. SNH – Loch Maree Islands.
Nr Kinlochewe, Tel 01445 760254

52. Loch Shiel Cruises.
Glenfinnan, Tel 01687 470322
www.highlandcruises.co.uk

53. RSPB – Nigg Bay.
Nigg, Tel 01463 715000

54. Northcoast Marine Adventures.
Nr Thurso, Tel 01955 611797
www.northcoast-marine-adventures.co.uk

55. Phoenix Boat Trips.
Nairn, Tel 01667 456078
www.greentourism.org.uk/Phoenix.html

56. Raasay Forest.
Isle of Raasay, Tel 01320 366322
www.forestry.gov.uk/scotland

57. SNH – Rassal Ashwood.
Kishorn, Tel 01445 760254

58. Ray Nowicki Wildlife Guide.
Nethybridge,
Tel 01479 821215 / 07743 182882

59. Rothiemurchus Estate.
Aviemore, Tel 01479 810858
www.rothiemurchus.net

60. Rua Reidh Lighthouse.
Gairloch, Tel 01445 771263
www.ruareidh.co.uk

61. SNH – Rum.
Tel 01687 462026

62. Sea-fari Adventures – Skye.
Armadale, Isle of Skye,
Tel 01471 833316
www.seafari.co.uk/skye

63. Seaprobe Atlantis – Glass Bottom Boat Trips.
Kyle of Lochalsh,
Tel 0800 980 4846
www.seaprobeatlantis.com

64. Shin Falls.
Lairg, Tel 01862 810359
www.forestry.gov.uk/scotland

65. Speyside Wildlife.
Inverdruie Nr Aviemore,
Tel 01479 812498
www.speysidewildlife.co.uk

66. FCS – Slattadale.
between Gairloch/Kinlochewe,
Tel 01463 791575
www.forestry.gov.uk/scotland

67. Special Boating Trips.
Mallaig, Tel 01687 462652
www.road-to-the-isles.org.uk

68. Speyside Wildlife.
– Day Guides & Evening
Wildlife Watching, Aviemore,
Tel 01479 812498
www.speysidewildlife.co.uk

69. Summer Queen Cruises.
Ullapool, Tel 01854 612472
www.summerqueen.co.uk

70. NTS – Torridon.
Nr Kinlochewe, Tel 01445 791368

71. The Corrour Trust.
Nr Fort William, Tel 01397 732200

72. Wildshots.
Glenfeshie, Kingussie,
Tel 01540 651 352
www.wildshots.co.uk

The Outer Hebrides

1. Adventure Hebrides.
Isle of Lewis, Tel 01851 820726
www.AdventureHebrides.com

2. RSPB – Balranald.
North Uist, Tel 01463 715000

3. Engebret Ltd.
Stornoway, Tel 01851 702304
www.visithebrides.co.uk

4. SNH – Loch Druidibeg.
South Uist, Tel 01870 620238

5. SNH – Monach Isles.
Western Isles, Tel 01870 620238

6. SNH – Rona and Sula Sgeir.
Western Isles, Tel 01851 705258

7. Scenic Cruises.
Flodabay, Isle of Harris,
Tel 01859 530310
www.scenic-cruises.co.uk

8. Seatrek.
Uig, Isle of Lewis,
Tel 01851 672464
www.seatrek.co.uk

9. NTS – St Kilda.
50 miles west of Outer Hebrides,
Tel 01463 232034
www.kilda.org.uk

10. VisitHebrides.
Stornoway, Tel 01851 703088
www.visithebrides.com

The Northern Isles –
Orkney and Shetland

1. **RSPB – Brodgar**.
   Stenness, Orkney,
   Tel 01856 850176
2. **RSPB – Cottascarth
   & Rendall Moss**.
   Orkney, Tel 01856 850176
3. **NTS – Fair Isle**.
   Shetland, Tel 01463 232034
4. **RSPB – Fetlar**.
   Shetland, Tel 01957 733246
5. **SNH – Hermaness**.
   Unst, Shetland, Tel 01595 693345
6. **RSPB – Hoy**.
   Orkney, Tel 01856 791298
7. **Hoy Ranger Service**.
   Hoy, Orkney, Tel 01856 791298
   www.orkneycommunities/co.uk/
   hoyrangerservice
8. **Island Trails**.
   Bigton, Shetland,
   Tel 01950 422408
   www.island-trails.co.uk
9. **Keen of Hamar**.
   Unst, Shetland, Tel 01595 693345
   www.nnr-scotland.org.uk
10. **RSPB – Marwick Head**.
    Stromness, Orkney,
    Tel 01856 850176
11. **RSPB – Mousa**.
    Island off mainland Shetland,
    Tel 01950 460800
12. **SNH – Noss**.
    Bressay, Shetland,
    Tel 0800 107 7818

13. **Orcadian Wildlife**.
    South Ronaldsay,
    Tel 01856 831240
    www.orcadianwildlife.co.uk
14. **Roving Eye Enterprises**.
    Orphir, Orkney,
    Tel 01856 811360
    www.rovingeye.co.uk
15. **Seabirds-and-Seals**.
    Bressay, Shetland,
    Tel 01595 693434
    www.seabirds-and-seals.com
16. **Shetland Wildlife**.
    Maywick, Shetland,
    Tel 01950422483
    www.shetlandwildlife.co.uk
17. **RSPB – Sumbergh Head**,
    Shetland, Tel 01950 460800
18. **RSPB – Trumland**,
    Rousay, Orkney,
    Tel 01856 850176

Wildlife Holidays Throughout Scotland
(Not numbered on map.)

Aigas Quest Ltd.
Beauly, Tel 01463782443
www.aigus.co.uk

CNDo Scotland.
Stirling, Tel 01786 445703
www.cndoscotland.com

Contours Walking Holidays.
Greystoke, Tel 017684 80451
www.contours.co.uk

**Guideliner Hebridean
Wildlife Cruises**.
Snizort, Isle of Skye,
Tel 01470 532393
www.guideliner.co.uk

**Land Rover Experience
Heatherlea (Scotland Ltd)**.
Nethybridge, Tel 01479 821248
www.heatherlea.co.uk

Island Holiday Plus.
Cumrie, Tel 01764 670107
www.islandholidays.co.uk

Scotland.
Dunkeld, Tel 01350 727720
www.wildperthshire.com

McKinlay Kidd Ltd.
Edinburgh, Tel 08707 606027
www.seescotlanddifferntly.co.uk
Email robert@mackinleykidd.co.uk

Natureguide (Travel) Ltd.
Dunfermline, Tel 01383 625874

Northern Light Charters.
Duror of Appin, Tel 01631 740595
www.northernlight-uk.com

Rob Roy Tours Ltd.
Edinburgh, Tel 01620 890908
www.RobRoyTours.com

Speyside Wildlife.
– Guided Wildlife Holidays,
Aviemore, Tel 01479 812498
www.speysidewildlife.co.uk

Wilderness Scotland.
Edinburgh, Tel 0131 625 6635
www.wildernessscotland.com

Visit Scotland
www.visitscotland.com/wildlife

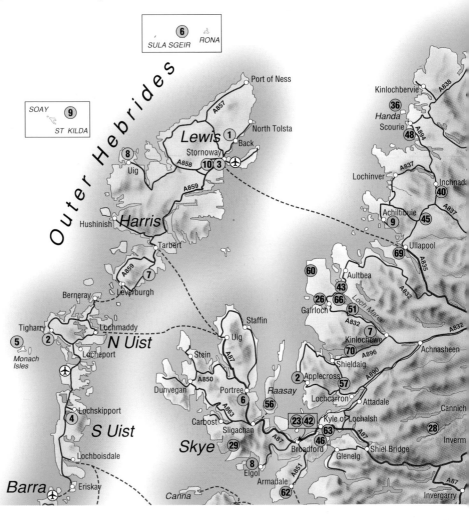

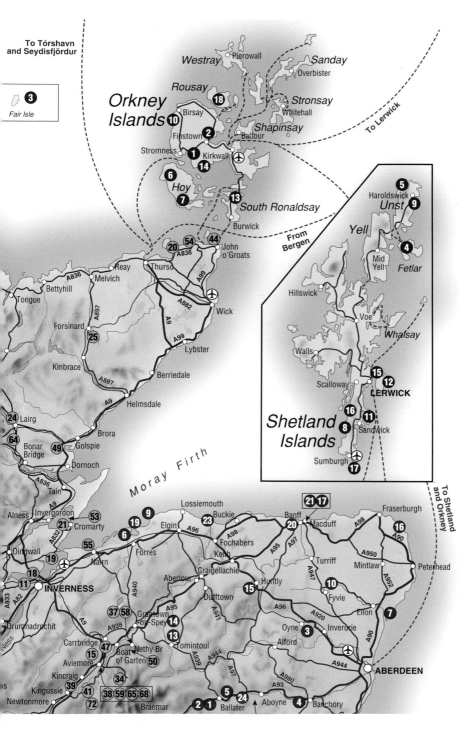

To Tórshavn
and Seydisfjördur

Fair Isle ③

Westray ○Pierowall
Rousay
Sanday ○Overbister
Orkney
Islands ⑩ ○Birsay
○Finstown ② ○Balfour Shapinsay
Stronsay
○Whitehall

Stromness○ ① ○Kirkwall
⑥ ⑭ ✈
Hoy ⑦
⑬
South Ronaldsay
○Burwick

Sanday

To Lerwick

From Bergen

⑤
Haroldswick
Unst ⑨
⑩ Finstown
Yell ④
Mid Yell Fetlar

Hillswick○

○Voe
Whalsay

Walls○

⑮ ○Scalloway ⑫
LERWICK

Shetland
Islands ⑯ ⑪
⑧ ○Sandwick

Sumburgh ✈
⑰

⑤④ ○John o'Groats
⑳ ○A836
○Reay ○Thurso
○Melvich
Bettyhill
Tongue○ A897
○Forsinard
②⑤
Kinbrace
A897
Helmsdale

○Berriedale

A9
Lybster○

✈ ○Wick

A882

A99

②④ ○Lairg
⑥④
Bonar Bridge ④⑨ ○Golspie
○Brora

○Dornoch
A836
○Tain
Alness○ A9
○Invergordon
②① ○Cromarty ⑤③
○Dingwall ⑤⑤
①⑨ ✈ ○Nairn
○Drumnadrochit
①⑧
①① INVERNESS

Moray Firth

○Lossiemouth ⑨
②① ⑰
○Buckie ○Banff ○Fraserburgh
⑲ ⑥ ○Elgin A96 ②③ Fochabers A98 ⑳ ○Macduff A98 ⑯
○Forres A95 A97 ○Turriff A950 ○Mintlaw ○Peterhead
○Keith A947 A952
○Craigellachie ○Fyvie ⑩
○Aberlour ⑮ ○Huntly
③⑦⑤⑧ ○Grantown-on-Spey ○Dufftown A96 A920 ○Inverurie ○Ellon ⑦
A940 ⑭ A941 ○Oyne ③ A90
○Carrbridge ⑬ ○Tomintoul ○Alford
⑮ ④⑦ Boat of Garten ⑤⓪ A939 ○Aboyne ④ ○Banchory
○Aviemore A944 ✈
○Kincraig ③④ A93 ABERDEEN
○Kingussie ③⑨
○Newtonmore ④① ③⑧⑤⑨⑥⑤⑥⑧
⑦② ○Braemar ② ① ⑤ ②④ ○Ballater

29

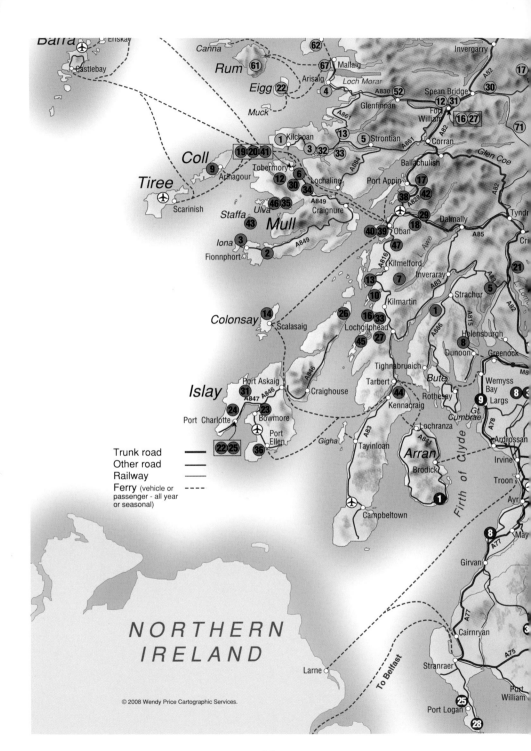

Barra
Eriskay
Castlebay
Canna
Rum
61
Eigg 22
Muck
62
67 Mallaig
Arisaig
Loch Morar
4
A830 52
Glenfinnan
A861
Invergarry
A82
17
Spean Bridge
12 31
Fort William
16 27
30
71

Coll
Tiree
9 Arinagour
19 20 41
1 Kilchoan
Tobermory
12
6
30 34
Lochaline
3 32
33
13
5 Strontian
A861
A884
Corran
A82
Ballachulish
Glen Coe
A82
Port Appin
17
38
42
A828
Dalmally
A85
Tyndrum
Crianlarich

Scarinish
46 35
Ulva
A849
Craignure
Staffa
43
Mull
Iona 3
Fionnphort
2
A849
40 39 Oban
29
18
47
Kilmelford
L. Awe
A816
13
7
Inveraray
A83
Strachur
5
A815
21
Kilmartin

Colonsay
14
Scalasaig
10
Kilmartin
26
16 33
Lochgilphead
45
27
1
A886
Helensburgh
8
Dunoon
Greenock
M8

Islay
Port Askaig
31
A847
A846
Craighouse
Bute
Tighnabruaich
Tarbert
44
Rothesay
Largs
Wemyss Bay
8
24
23 Bowmore
Port Charlotte
Port Ellen
36
Gigha
Kennacraig
Gt. Cumbrae
9
Ardrossan
Irvine
Troon
8
Ayr
22 25
Tayinloan
Lochranza
A841
Arran
Brodick
1
Firth of Clyde

Campbeltown

Trunk road
Other road
Railway
Ferry (vehicle or
passenger - all year
or seasonal)

NORTHERN
IRELAND

8 May
Girvan

Larne
Cairnryan
A77
A75
Stranraer
Port William
25
Port Logan
28

© 2008 Wendy Price Cartographic Services.

31

DISCOVER SCOTLAND'S
SEA EAGLES AND WILDCATS

The White-tailed or Sea eagle was reintroduced to Scotland from Norway. Between 1975 and 1985, 82 chicks were released on the Isle of Rum. Initially they didn't nest there but wandered south to Mull and north to Skye, other islands, and the mainland. The first nest with a chick to fledge was on Mull in 1985. Between 1992 and 1998, 58 chicks were alsoreleased in Wester Ross. Now Scotland has 43+ pairs, and during 2007, 34 chicks were fledged. You can discover Sea eagles with 'Mull Eagle Watch' in a ranger-led visit to a special hide at Loch Frisa on the Isle of Mull. The two hour visits are very popular and must be booked in advance. Tel 01688 302038 www.rspb.org.uk/brilliant/sites/mull/index.asp

The Scottish Wildcat , *Felis silvestris grampia*, is now so rare that it is estimated only 400 exist in the wild, making it the rarest mammal in the UK. Found in the most remote, sparsely populated areas of the Scottish Highlands, they are twice the size of a domestic cat. Although they were once common persecution over the last two centuries, especially by gamekeepers, has endangered this sub-species. Wildcats have interbred with domestic cats creating fertile hybrids, so in order to conserve pure wildcats and to save the species from extinction the newly formed **Scottish Wildcat Association** has initiated a conservation breeding programme. Wildcats can be seen in captivity in Scotland at venues involved in the Scottish Wildcat Association's breeding programme, – The Highland Wildlife Park, Kingussie, Inverness-shire www.highlandwildlifepark.org, and Five Sisters Zoo, West Lothian www.fivesisterszoo.co.uk For more information about the conservation work of the Scottish Wildcat Association, and to view wonderful photographs of this elusive mammal, plus a video, visit their website www.scottishwildcats.co.uk

SEA WATCH

From blue depths a solitary minke surfaced for air. A full grown male, he had emerged every half hour, creating a wake of silver circles in the moonlit sea. He followed a faint chemical trace of herring south from the Small Isles as he passed Ardnamurchan Point. Emerging from one of Mull's western sea lochs, a basking shark tasted the water with a 'nose' sensitive to stimuli it detected. Alert to minute traces, and electrical changes in the ocean, she orientated a course towards Gunna Sound where she 'smelt' - plankton. In the west, on the Treshnish Isles and Coll and Tiree, drowsy seabirds awakened and fluffed out their feathers. On Mull's northern coast a whale research boat rocked at anchor, its whale watchers ashore, asleep.

Sunrise streaked the sea orange, promising summer heat to warm the Hebridean Sea whose surface had steadily absorbed solar energy producing a warm layer above cold depths below. This boded well for all these sea watchers. The minke and basking shark, each pursuing sensory messages were not rivals but different consumers in the vast, sun dependent, marine food web. An algal bloom occurred each spring, with increased sunlight, and nutrients in the cold water now fed billions of microscopic aquatic animals creating rich organic nutrient at the sea surface. Now this 'soup' of plankton attracted herring, keen to utilise summer's bounty.

A school of herring, a changing silvery shape, had fed voraciously during the night, shimmering moonlight concealing their presence. No predators attacked, so the herring formed loose swarms swimming with mouths open, sieving plankton through their gills. As day dawned they bunched, a school of thousands, swimming in perfect unison. Sensitive to vibrations, sound pulses from their bodies, and to light flashed from silvered scales when turning, they were perfectly synchronised.

The minke whale, a regular visitor to the Hebrides, rhythmically surfacing and diving, followed their trail. Its hairless body was scarred from squid attack and its sickle shaped dorsal fin nicked where a killer whale had savagely bitten it as a calf. Protected then by his mother, he now lived a virtually solitary life. By contrast the basking shark, with no maternal care, was a natural survivor. Nine metres long and weighing five tonnes it was impervious to disease. A harmless filter feeder nothing threatened, - except man. Hourly enough water to fill two Olympic sized swimming pools passed through its gills.

The whale watchers had finished breakfast and packed their bags with binoculars and cameras, ready for the boat. Meanwhile the minke was swimming towards the Cairns of Coll, 'blow' from its nostrils a gentle 'sigh' over the quiet sea. The basking shark passed the Isle of Staffa towards the Dutchman's Hat and Lunga, whilst the school of herring hid in deep water between the Treshnish Isles and Coll, but an oily molecular film of herring protein on the sea surface left a tell-tale fingerprint of their presence. In the drifting plankton microscopic animals ate anything vulnerable that they came across. Insensible to anything except the sun lighting and warming the surface water, microscopic algae converted sunlight into food.

The whale research boat sped to an area favoured by visiting minkes as watchers, stationed around the top deck, scanned sectors of sea, hopeful for sightings. Sounds from the boat's engines carried through the water to the whale's ears buried deep inside its vast head. Recognising the familiar sound it wasn't unduly perturbed. What interested it most were the stronger trace of herring oil it had encountered, and the taste of plankton. Deep below he knew there was food in abundance.

Emerging between the Dutchman's Hat and Lunga the basking shark sensed the 'smell' was stronger northwards. Opening her huge mouth she swam north oblivious to anything except an appetite for plankton. Mouth agape and gill slits open, sieving an increasing volume of plankton, she torpedoed blindly onwards - on a collision course.

The whale surfaced for air, its back and curved dorsal fin breaking the surface, before disappearing. The whale watcher's boat was stationary, the engine cut. Seabirds quartered the area searching for fish. A whale watcher pointed westwards in excitement. 'A minke fin broke the surface, - way over there!' We'll follow, but we mustn't unduly disturb or stress it' said the captain, restarting the engines.

The minke dived deep leaving the bright sunlit surface. From 50 metres down he swam towards increasingly dark blue depths. He knew food lurked somewhere, but where? He was very hungry. So too was the basking shark but her appetite was slowly being satiated. Ploughing a shallow furrow through the water, plankton were taken in and forced through five pairs of meter long gill slits. Intent upon swallowing the bounty trapped by her dovetailed gill-rakers, she didn't notice the speeding boat until it was almost on her. Too late she swerved and bounced, unharmed, down the starboard side. 'BASKING SHARK!' someone shouted, and everyone watched the harmless giant as she continued, unconcerned, on her feeding quest.

The herring in cold water below the surface warmth had not swum deep enough. They rested, loosely in contact, at 90 metres below the surface. Another 10 metres would have shielded them into total darkness, but the minke had sensed their vicinity and had seen the schools outer limit. Silently he dived deeper still, until well below them in the darkness, then turning, he surged upwards to the fish.

Surprised by their unseen predator the herring immediately headed away from the danger, towards the surface. The first fish there attracted the attention of seabirds that swooped ravenously, their raucous calls bringing in more birds. The sea surface boiled with fish trying to escape, whilst beneath them others rotated in a huge ball. Seabirds dived, stabbing with their beaks, gluttonously swallowing the silver bounty. But they scattered skywards, screaming, when the sea surface erupted in a wall of water, whale, and showers of fish. Breaching the surface, the minke's throat was so distended with herring that its throat grooves showed pink. 'LUNGE! 12 o'clock!' shouted a whale-watcher, and all on board rushed to see. Keeping their distance the watchers saw the minke take his fill three times more before finally diving and disappearing completely.

The watchers concentrated their attention on the same quarter, empty except for a few seabirds, when a long hiss issued behind them and an aroma of rotten cabbage was smelt. He had surfaced close to the boat's stern. Awed watchers were spellbound, the click of cameras breaking a tense silence. Swimming under and up again beneath their bows the whale reacquainted himself with this familiar object. To the watchers he looked like a huge tadpole as they recorded the white patterns on his pectoral fins and nicks on his damaged dorsal fin. Finally, inhaling deeply, he dived and was gone. 'He's an old friend' said the captain smiling.

To the north of Coll the basking shark still fed single-mindedly, barely noticing the common seal cow and calf she collided with; the sea surface sparkling brightly from the high sun. As she ploughed westwards, the minke passed Iona, whilst the whale watchers visited the common seal colony on the Cairns of Coll. The sun was sinking in a multi-hued sea beyond Tiree as they sped home, amply rewarded by their day's sea watch.

THE HUNGRY SEA EAGLE

The sea eagle watched a hooded crow opposite his eyrie pick the bones of a mountain hare that he'd discarded on the rocky knoll two days earlier. From his treetop in the lee of a vast ice-plucked crag, the three-year old male watched the crow with predatory interest. The sun was still behind the mountains and he was hidden in shadow. If this carrion-eater was to become his breakfast, the sea eagle knew he would have to surprise it, for the wily crow would fly if it detected sudden movement. Gripping the branch with clawed yellow feet he poised for flight, hooked beak gaping, tongue licking the roof of his mouth. He keenly scrutinised the crow. He was hungry.

At the moment the sun's rays pierced the skyline the sea eagle leapt. The brightness concealed him but the beat of his huge wings alerted the crow who dropped the carcass and fled, cawing raucously. The sea eagle gradually gained on his prey as the crow flew down into the glen where it habitually perched on the telephone cable opposite a small cottage, where it raided the bird table. Now the cunning bird sought sanctuary between the insulators on the telegraph pole where it cawed stridently. A woman walking her dog in the fields, saw above her the wide silhouette and unmistakeable white tail of the sea eagle. Unconcerned by the barking dog, the predator circled, watching the crow. Finally, defeated by the crafty bird, the eagle emitted a high-pitched call, and beat his two metre wide wings, ascending the hillside opposite towards northern hills.

Undeterred by failure the sea eagle flew above the boggy treads and rocky risers of the stepped tableland beneath him, now lit by rosy dawn. There were ground nesting birds to be found here, rabbits and hares. Sheep were grazing below, nibbling grass washed by a night of rain after a long spring drought. Nimble lambs closely followed their shaggy mothers. Flying higher he scouted for any tell-tale patch of white against the green. Stillborn lambs, though skinny, made an adequate meal. All he found was the remains left by a golden eagle – pecked clean by crows! Cresting the hills, the sea around the island of Ulva looked like beaten metal in the bright sun. Soaring on up-draughts he noted a straggle of people hurrying towards a motorboat at the jetty. Keeping to high ground, the young sea eagle winged north, intent upon patrolling the summits overlooking Mull's Loch Tuath.

Golden plovers nesting the hill tops crouched protectively over their chicks as he flew overhead. In a rocky hollow he spotted a solitary red deer with her newborn calf. The hind watched warily as he landed, hoping for a meal of afterbirth but she had already eaten it. Intimidated by the sea eagle the hind moved off, her calf staggering to its feet and following on wobbly legs. He watched them go before excited yelping commanded his attention, seeing near the south end of Ulva, cart-wheeling aerial display of mature sea eagles' courting. He watched them collide in mid-air, their talons grappling each other. The female, lighter in colour, larger and heavier, seemed the dominant one. Wiser not to fly that way into possible conflict he preened his dark brown feathers until a solitary sea gull flew over the hill top, and the young eagle took off to follow.

Sea gulls made good meals. Realising it was being pursued the gull flew faster but the eagle gained and was soon close enough to grab the bird. Innately agile, the gull dropped to the safety of the seashore far below. The sea eagle dived after it. Flying over a rocky headland he was within a talons grasp of catching it when three greater black-backed gulls pecking at something large on the shore distracted him when they took off in alarm. The smell of rotting flesh from a young porpoise washed up on the narrow, rocky beach offered an easier meal. Keeping away from the advancing tide he continued the scavenging work started by the black-backs. Tearing off chunks of flesh with his hooked beak he ate quickly for waves were lapping the carcass. Too soon he was forced to fly away, before the tide left him no beach from which to take off.

With powerful, ponderous wing beats he flew high over Loch Tuath. Around the north of Ulva he saw the Staffa motorboat returning. In the bright sunshine the Treshnish Isles looked vivid green. Deciding not investigate Lunga, where he sometimes caught unwary puffins leaving their burrows, he rode the thermals rising above the warm black basalt rocks of the island. Circling higher and higher, his horizontal and primary wing feathers spread wide, he surveyed the scene. Far below flashes of sunlight reflected from binoculars trained upon him from the motorboat as he soared, swooped, and rose, circling the heights. Crowding the open deck, watchers on the boat followed his majestic flight.

The trippers had driven away in their cars before the sea eagle winged homeward again. Following the coast this time he turned eastwards into Loch na Keal. He had almost reached the head of the loch when he saw, on rocks near a sandy bay, a family of otters. Otters meant the chance of another meal for they often caught more fish than they consumed and obligingly left uneaten remains ashore. He could see an adult otter and two cubs and he watched overhead as the adult and one cub swam away leaving the other by the rocks. He was about to land to chase this cub away when a car pulled up and two people got out. He saw them watching him, so he circled, waiting, witnessing commotion as their dog caught the remaining cub, then drop it and the creature escape. Watching the otter family swim away he saw a larger otter join them. Noticing the people's attention fixed now on the bay, he swooped down and retrieved the barely eaten remains of a flatfish. Only the dog saw him, and growled, its hackles bristling.

The sea eagle took off with powerful wing beats clutching a plaice. Flying over stunted woodland, open grassland, and hill tops of the southern mountains, he arrived back at his favourite eyrie. Soaring over the huge crag he hovered above the cliff edge, and landed, very gently, in his tree.

THE TURN OF THE TIDE

The shore crab edged itself from the protective crevice on the tide-covered shore. The wind driven waves of the night had calmed and the sea now reflected dawn's pink glow. A full moon had pulled the tide higher up the shore, wetting tar-black lichens on the rocks. Now it was falling, exposing short rubbery fronds of green-brown channel wrack to become dehydrated, black and brittle if the day remained dry. Minute periwinkles, and larger ones with rough, grey pointed shells, had tucked themselves into tiny cracks and shut their shells to avoid desiccation. The shore crab didn't care for these small snails or the green woodlouse-like ocean-slaters that roamed the splash zone, so he never ventured to the shore top for such poor pickings. Instead he roamed the middle and lower shore where, with his green shell the colour of the seaweed that clung thickly to the rocks, he was camouflaged and could survive more easily.

Close to the landward limits of his territory, the mature male scurried between fronds of spiral wrack twisting in the tide's ebb and flow. Limpets glided back home, rasping encrusting algae with file-like tongues from the smooth rock, as they returned to sucker down on their own oval depression. On the middle shore, some were already secure, their head, tentacles, and muscular foot hidden within their steep conical shell. Knowing the impossibility of attacking those fixed to the rock the crab waited amongst weed hoping to ambush any unwary creatures in the vicinity. His mouthparts moved mechanically in expectation. Too slow to catch a transparent shrimp whose long antennae accidentally touched his own, a homeward-bound limpet, meandering around the holdfasts of spiral wrack, was a victim instead. The crab's sharp pincers shot outwards, missing the limpet's small head but nipping a tentacle. Instantly the shell clamped down and despite his agitated attempts proved impossible for the shore crab to budge. Encrusting barnacles filtering food from sea water were alerted by the commotion, immediately withdrawing their tiny jointed legs and closing their shutter-like plates. Flicking his small five-jointed tail the crab backed away, disturbing plum-red beadlet anemones that quickly withdrew their tentacles inside their sac-like bodies. The hungry crab swam to knotted-wrack whose egg-like bladders buoyed the leathery fronds erect. In deeper water now where the rocks gave way to sand, he was in a veritable forest of seaweed that swayed gently as the tide retreated.

Variedly coloured flat periwinkles, green, brown, yellow, and orange, grazed the knotted and bladder wrack that grew in this shore zone. The crab needed all the enhanced eyesight that his compound eyes offered to detect the snails because their rounded shells with flattened spires, coloured like the bladders of the seaweed, hid them perfectly. Expertly climbing knotted wrack, his four pairs of back legs rested delicately on swollen reproductive nodules ripe with eggs soon to be shed. Immobile he hid behind a festoon of polyzoa, tiny plant-like animals growing on the frond. The tide was steadily dropping when a large orange snail glided back down the lengthy frond whose tip now lay on the surface. Infinitely carefully the crab manoeuvred his pincers into position to intercept the flat periwinkle, its vulnerable head-foot within the crab's sharp sight. As it passed pincers flashed out from the concealed crab and the tentacles and head of the unwary snail were gripped fast. Its soft flesh was quickly and fastidiously devoured, by slicing movements of the crab's armoured mouthparts. The discarded shell sank to join other empty shells on a patch of sand below. Unobserved, a tiny hermit crab living inside a smaller periwinkle shell dragged himself over to the new shell, inspecting it carefully before quickly transferring his soft body into this larger home. Shuffling back to the shelter of overhanging rock the hermit shut his 'front door' provided by his armoured pincers.

Scuttling down the weed the still hungry shore crab made its way between fronds of bladder-wrack and through serrated saw-wrack to a raft of mussels clinging by their tough threads to a rocky edge. Two dog whelks, siphons waving alongside their brown and white-banded spires, glided away satiated. Tell-tale holes neatly drilled in now empty mussel shells showed which they had eaten. A common starfish was dining, its suckered arms clamped on one of the blue-black molluscs, pulling the two shells apart. The crab examined the mussel bed looking for any that might have been damaged the night before. Gaping slightly as their frilly-edged siphons filtered food particles suspended in the water, the mussel's valves shut abruptly as he tip-toed over them. But he was in luck. At the edge of the colony were two mussels with smashed shells, their flesh still inside. Pulling out pieces of creamy-coloured mussel he was feasting on one when a menacing shape loomed before him. It was a female shore crab! Larger, with a seven-jointed tail and bigger pincers raised aggressively, the female moved towards him in a threatening manner. Instinctively he raised his pincers but as she advanced he backed away. Leaving the remaining mussel, he dropped to the sand below, scuttling sideways to a rock festooned in seaweed by the receding tide. Thick-shelled edible winkles were still grazing as the crab tucked himself under a protective curtain and furtively watched as the marauding female, her stolen meal finished, selected the same rock for shelter. The tide had reached the leathery brown kelp and left the shore exposed to the warm sun.

Protected from drying amongst moist saw-wrack the male crab endured exposure as the day warmed. A spring tide, with all the shore uncovered, he would be out of water for a longer time. Occasionally bubbles burst from between his mouthparts, whilst the winkles with which he shared his shelter emitted little sounds as they adjusted the opercula that closed their shells. Through a gap between the draping seaweed he saw a stretch of sand worth investigating for worms when the tide turned and he was no longer vulnerable. Suddenly he was aware of vigorous activity. The weed cloaking the rock was being shaken!

A large otter nosing under the weed emerged with the female shore crab in her mouth. The male crab saw the otter drop her onto the sand, and he watched as she raised her pincers, before scuttling sideways. Two smaller otters pounced, playing with her briefly before one bit the brittle shell. The male crab shrank back amongst the fronds. Unable to escape whilst the tide was out he was totally vulnerable. A bristly, inquisitive face penetrated the weed. He raised his pincers in self-defence but was pulled triumphantly from hiding by a young otter. The returning tide lifted the kelp and advanced again towards the rocks. But it had turned too late for the shore crab.

THE OYSTERCATCHER FAMILY

The faint gold-grey hint of dawn glowed beyond distant silhouetted mountains as the oystercatcher awoke and ruffled her feathers. Under her protective breast two tiny chicks stirred drowsily. Turing the one un-hatched egg, she called to her mate on his false nest nearby, her quiet 'weep-weep' mingling with the lap of the falling tide. After his reassuring high-pitched 'kleep' she contented herself with rearranging the bedraggled nest edge. Set in a sheltered rocky hollow above the high tide mark of a small offshore island, the site was well chosen. The nest was walled by twisted seaweed and decorated with pebbles and broken shells. A sandy isthmus connected the isle with a vast sandy bay. Less than one full moon previously she had courted in the bay, dancing with her flock of 'sea-pies' in a communal mating display. Head lowered and bill tip almost touching the fine sand, she had peeped excitedly with the others. Now, courtship over and their nest territory established, they already had two hungry bills to feed.

Standing up she straightened her long pink legs, stretched her pointed black wings with their white bar, and surveyed the bay. Rosy rays between the distant peaks now reflected on waves rolling gently shore-wards. The tide had dropped below the tufted brown channel wrack, uncovering sand to be foraged. Soon the winter-cooled sea would withdraw from the buoyant bladder wrack, revealing a plentiful larder. Her fluffy-downed chicks raised their short bills, stumpy wings flapping. She coaxed them to settle back into the protection of the nest, and leaving her mate standing guard, she flew off with strong, shallow wing beats.

She was not alone when she landed on the sands. Other wading birds were gathering, many already probing the wet ooze with their bills. Plunging her 'stabber' bill deeply near a tell-tale squiggle of sandy-mud she withdrew gripping a small, wriggling lugworm. By the rocks hammer-billed oystercatchers attacked rafts of mussels attached to the rocks by short strong threads. Limpets uncovered as the tide withdrew were taken unawares before they could sucker down on their rocky base. Swallowing her fat worm the mother oystercatcher probed the sand for tellinids – small bivalves with pearly, translucent shells and succulent orange flesh. Finding three in quick succession she adroitly stabbed the delicate valves apart and scooped out the flesh. Gripping this in her bill tip, she took off to feed her young.

As she arrived her mate departed, whilst her chicks stood on quivering blue-grey legs, tiny bills agape. Filling their hungry mouths she settled down on the nest again for a lone blotchy olive-brown egg needed her warmth. Surveying her territory for predators she noted a small boat far across the bay. She also kept a watchful eye for her returning mate and some minutes later he alighted on rocks near the water's edge before trotting rapidly to the nest. He had knocked limpets from the rocks and whilst he fed these to the young she flew off again.

Having satisfied her own appetite with the flesh of a fat cockle she'd dug from the sand, discarding the gaping shell, she returned to the nest with more. As her mate departed towards a small islet offshore, she noted as she turned their last egg that the speckled shell was cracked.

The sky was a deeper blue and distant islands brilliant green shapes above the sea as black-backed gulls soaring on the morning breeze, scanned the shoreline near the oystercatcher's nest with beady yellow eyes. The mother bird crouched over her chicks, watching the gluttonous gulls spying out their breakfast. Wisely they left her nest alone, preferring easier prey. Instead she turned her fierce, protective instinct towards a passing curlew that innocently approached too close. Returning from her swift mobbing flight she found a small hole in the egg. Calling encouragement to her unborn chick she briefly watched its beak moving within the confines of its shell before settling down and fluffing out her breast feathers.

The boat she had spotted in the distance chugged closer across the bay. A few hopeful gulls followed it as it headed towards the island. At the tip of the rocky isle its engine idled as it rose and sank on the swell. The oystercatcher saw a splash as something large hit the water and disappeared. A bright orange ball bobbed on the surface. The boat moved closer. She saw two men and heard their voices above the dull chug of the engine. Alarmed at their proximity she took off peeping wildly, her mate joining her on the wing. They flew around the boat calling shrilly before flying back low over the sea, their wingtips almost touching the water. The lobster fishermen unconcernedly dropped another creel before revving the boat engine to steer a course around the other side of the island. Having left the nest to avert any possible danger the concerned pair returned to check that all was still well. But something had happened, the nest looked different. Broken shell fragments cluttered the hollow where the two fluffy chicks crouched immobile. Standing beside them on wobbly legs its bedraggled feathers still flattened and moist, was the third chick.

The oystercatcher family was now complete. Glossy brown kelp stipes emerged from the receding tide, their leathery straps glinting on the sea surface brilliant in the noonday sunshine. The air was warm and unusually still when the mother oystercatcher flew off yet again to gather food for her family. With another insatiable mouth to feed she needed to probe the sands for as much food as she could find before the returning tide covered it again. Her tranquil 'kleep-kleep', called as she left her mate, floated across the sandy isthmus and carried to the end of the bay.

AT THE EDGE OF THE ATLANTIC

Dawn silhouetted distant mountaintops when the cow seal awoke after the shortest night of summer. A full moon had pulled the tide higher and waves lapped at the rocks on which she and her pup lay. The rookery was crowded with female common seals and their young. Once plump from extra feeding during April and May, most had given birth early in June. Suckling their pups gave them a sleeker shape, as they produced fat-rich milk that nourished their fast-growing young. The hungry mother of many seasons looked out over the unusually calm sea deciding that today she must feed, and she would take her male pup on his first foray beyond the protection of the rocky Cairns.

Other cows, their spotted coats blending with the rocks, were already moving their pups higher. Open-mouthed she hissed at one moving too close, flapping a stiff, clawed, fore flipper defensively. The other female and pup selected an empty area well beyond her reach, but she watched them, as well as scanning the sea area for any possible danger. Her three week-old pup stirred and she nudged it with her dog-like nose. Hungrily the pup pushed his blunt face under her tail, finding one of the two nipples buried in her soft fur. Lying on her side she murmured to him as he sucked first one, then the other nipple, switching repeatedly until he'd had his fill. Then she wriggled from her rocky perch and slipped into the clear water where she dived and circled gracefully. Emerging, with wet whiskers and shining fur, she called and her pup slipped down over the rocky ledge to join her. Two female pups, whose mothers' had left them in the protection of the rookery whilst they hunted food, were chasing each other in calm water between rocky crags. The male pup joined them for a game – 'porpoising' in joyous leaps across the water. She watched the three splashing and rolling, creating surface bubbles as their spotted streamlined bodies became silvered by trapped air when they dived to the sandy bottom. Leaving them playing, she submerged to nose rocky crevices searching for anything edible. Her whiskered muzzle detected the short antennae of a crab that tried, unsuccessfully, to wedge itself further into the crack.

With the taste of crab in her mouth, she called to her pup. The weather looked set fair for his first swim outside the rookery. She knew it wouldn't be long before he was weaned and would have to fend for himself. Her pup was on a rock, about to chase a pup into the water when, hearing her call, he slithered off and swam to join her. The two female pups watched as he swam away and one rolled over and smacked the water with her flipper to entice him back to play. Instead he followed his mother through a slithery brown forest of swaying kelp fronds and together they swam through this 'doorway' to the open sea.

Taking him around the outer edge of the rookery she dived to show him fish and invertebrates that lived amongst the rocks. Sunlight refracted through the water, lighting submarine cliffs encrusted in anemones, sponges, starfish, fan-worms, sea squirts, barnacles and sea urchins. A small octopus, eight suckered legs outstretched, was surprised before it could retreat to its crevice. She seized it in her mouth, showing it to her pup, before consuming it whole. They surfaced and she led him away to open sea, her

pup surfacing and diving at her side. In the distance she saw a flurry of gulls diving. Knowing this meant a plentiful supply of fish at the surface, she changed course, guiding her pup at his steady pace towards the activity. The flocking gulls wheeled and screamed whilst the sea surface 'boiled' with fish driven up to the surface. Wary of danger, she stopped and saw a minke whale surface, and lunge at the bait ball of herring, sending the raucous gulls skywards. Relieved that it was a minke, she dived with her pup, taking him towards the rotating silver ball of tightly packed fish driven up by the whale. Waiting at a safe distance they saw the huge dark whale rise from the depths to lunge, open-mouthed, at the fish ball again. Its white throat distended and fleshy grooves showed red as it submerged, scattering escaping fish. Showing her prowess underwater, the cow sped after escaping herring, swimming back to her pup with one in her teeth to show him before she swallowed it whole. She caught more with bursts of speed, a forward thrust of her neck and snapping jaws, until her stomach was full at last. She was glad her pup was interested in her hunt for food and had safely observed his first whale – whilst learning to keep a respectful distance! She knew that minke whales did not threaten seals, but her pup would be lucky to be warned in advance about the seal-eating killer whale, Orca, that hunted in this area.

Heading west she hauled up with her pup on an islet. The tide had fallen exposing a strip of white shell-sand. The sun was now high and the sand warm as she rolled over for her pup to suckle. When he'd finished she stretched, groomed, and rolled in the sand, her skin itchy as she approached the summertime moult. On another islet, not far away, she could hear the noises of bull seals and realised she would probably have to fend off males, desirous to mate, when they made their journey back to the rookery.

Deciding her best course of action was avoidance of the bull seals, she headed wide of the islets, yet in open water a young bull approached. Her pup at her side she dived and swam wide to avoid him, but he dived after her. Surfacing she barked stridently, clawing him when he approached. Her vociferous warnings attracted an older bull and before the amorous young bull could attempt to mate he had to fight. The bulls bit and slashed with their claws at each other's necks, creating pink-tinged foam with the intensity of their combat. The cow and pup hurriedly escaped, but as they dived, she saw a huge black and white shape moving towards the fighting bulls.

Swimming under water as fast as her pup could manage she distanced themselves before surfacing to look back. The sea was boiling in a frenzy of motion, and she watched, fearful, as the young bull was suddenly flung high above the waves, to be caught bodily in the open jaws of an Orca. Torpedoing away below the surface, she was terrified the killer whale would pursue them when it had finished playing with the body of the young male. Her pup keeping up, she made straight for the rookery, in her panic colliding with a huge basking shark that was harmlessly sieving plankton.

The tide was high again when they reached the rookery. Hauling up on in her usual site the cow lay still watching the sea for a few minutes before she rolled over and allowed her hungry pup some rich milk. Soon he would be weaned and on his own. She knew the day's experiences would stand him in good stead.

TAKING TO THE WATER

Dawn's rosy light lit the mossy boulders of the otter's holt. Snuggled beside her sleeping cubs the mother otter stirred in the confined nest. Her cubs – a male and a female, had grown large. Her sensitive nose prodded their thickly furred bodies before she wriggled out to assess the day. Peering short-sightedly towards the loch her nose told her more about the morning than her eyes. It had rained heavily in the night and the air was washed clean. Amongst other information, her keen nose detected the smell of her mate, the large dog otter who had fed her and her cubs for two months since their birth. She had not seen him for a month since the cubs weaned. Snuggled contentedly and used to her morning hunt for food, the cubs were unaware that today would be any different.

Nudged awake, their high pitch whimpers anticipated breakfast. Puzzled that there wasn't any, the cubs scrambled after their mother, following as she slid down the wet path between small twisted oak, birch and rowan trees. Sliding was fun and she knew today's lessons must become games if she was to teach her cubs to swim. Scampering down the slope, longer back legs arching her body, she whistled shrilly. Her cubs replied with high pitched piping sounds as, half hidden by tussocks, they followed. Pausing, she stood on hind legs and sniffed the air. The cubs clambered up a stump of bogwood where, during the night, their father had marked his territory – his black twisted spraint, shiny and fresh. They quickly lost interest in his musk preferring to slip between concealing tussocks to slide into the streambed where they sometimes played, – but the stream was swollen by the night's rain and the cubs hastily scrambled out – drenched. They chattered querulously, briskly shaking themselves, the dark guard hair of their pelts clumping into furry spikes. The mother otter nuzzled them encouragingly and led off again, following the stream towards the loch. This familiar route suited her purpose very well.

Naturally water-shy, the young otters found their unexpected soaking harmless and followed to where a shallow pool had filled. Here their mother rolled playfully, exposing her creamy underside, encouraging them to join her. Soon all three cavorted, wrestling and biting each other's tail tips as they chased back and forth across the pool. The sun was higher when she led them on, splashing together through riffles but swimming alone in the pools, her watching cubs chattering nervously. Eventually she led them under an arched road bridge. On the further side was a deep pool and into this she dived, disappearing without a ripple whilst they peered, quizzically, over the edge. Beneath the surface she gracefully circled, a path of bubbles rising from her fur.

With valves closing her nostrils, and hairs her small ears, but eyes wide open, she scouted for fish, muzzling every cranny, but nothing edible touched her sensitive whiskers. Submerged for two minutes in the silky water she surfaced to find her cubs piping distressfully. Emerging from the water sleek and wet she immediately butted them in! Buoyant with their baby under-fur they paddled frantically, the claws of their webbed feet clutching at the bank to escape. Scrambling out with undignified haste, they shook themselves, their thick under-fur still dry. Diving in again their mother called them to join her as she swam across the pool, but they ran across the rocks instead, leaving small webbed footprints. At the loch-side the stream braided into a pebbly delta, – a good place to catch fish on an incoming tide. But the tide was low and the mother otter led her cubs along the rocky shoreline piled high with seaweed as oystercatchers flew peeping overhead. Waves swashed up the beach and the cubs jumped in surprise, but becoming more confident, when they reached a sandy bay of cockleshells and weed covered rocks, they started to explore.

Pushing her whiskery head under festoons of knotted wrack their mother emerged triumphantly with a shore crab in her mouth. Holding it delicately in her paws, sharp canines crunched its carapace and she tore off pieces for her cubs to eat. Then she found another crab, deliberately dropping it. Initially immobile the crab suddenly scuttled sideways, so she pounced on it and then retreated. Inquisitively the cubs investigated as she backed off leaving them to pounce upon it, one of them experimentally biting it before dropping it quickly. The other took the injured prey and ate, its crunching noise encouraging the other to search under seaweed, whereupon it too grabbed a crab, and fed.

Emboldened, the cubs continued searching finding crabs as much a game as a means of satisfying hunger. The tide had turned and their mother, now in deep water, caught a large flatfish that she left ashore before catching another. Sharp canines gripping she emerged from the sea as her hungry cubs scampered to join her. Overhead a sea eagle, huge wings outspread, silhouetted the afternoon sky. Protected by rocks the mother otter tore pieces to share with her cubs, their molars noisily grinding the fish bones to pulp before swallowing. Then with a fleshy piece of tail she enticed her cubs into the water, lying on her back clutching her lure. As one clambered onto her belly intent on the fish tail she pushed off with her back legs, drifting into deeper water she submerged leaving her cub frantically paddling. Its calls of distress were echoed by its sibling crouching in a crevice on the shore. Emerging again, the mother otter called shrilly and her cub swam easily towards her. Just at that moment a car stopped by and people with a dog emerged, binoculars trained on the sky. Bounding to the water where it smelt out the cub in its hiding place the soft-mouthed dog captured it triumphantly. Shrill noises alerted the people who shouted at their dog, and he dropped his prize. The terrified (but unharmed) cub dashed to join the others, danger overcoming its fear of water; webbed feet finding their true element at last. As the people watched, a large dog otter, diving and surfacing in sinuous loops joined the family. Only their chastised pet saw a huge bird swoop down and wing away with the otter's fish in its talons.

THE RED SQUIRREL'S TALE

The red squirrel left her three young curled up asleep in the dray as she descended cautiously to the ground, to recover nuts stored nearby. It was almost dawn. Always on the alert for danger, her tufted ears heard before her sharp black eyes saw, a man approaching through the pine forest. Flattening her bushy tail and stretching it out behind her, she crouched low, watchful. The man carried a large rucksack and as he approached she ran up her Scots pine, her rusty-red fur matching its bark, whilst long, sharp, curved claws and strong hind legs sped her upwards to the safety of a branch. The man stopped directly beneath her, examining chewed pine cones littering the ground, before opening his bag. Balanced by her long tail she watched, incensed at his invasion of her territory. Petite, but bold, she dashed along the branch chattering angrily at him, ending with a few sharp barks! The man, seeing her agitated movements, smiled, picked up his bag, and moved on. She saw him unpack and leave its contents in a pile at the edge of a clearing before quietly returning the way he'd come. Secure again she scampered to the ground, nervously examined the pile of canvas, netting, and poles, and finding them harmless continued her feeding quest before returning to suckle her young.

The next day the man returned at the same time and moved the pile into the clearing. She watched from on high, her long heels on which she rested giving stability as she nibbled young green cones. She fluffed up her tail, secure in her Scots pine stronghold, but when he moved out of sight, ever inquisitive, she jumped to the next tree, her bushy tail acting as a parachute. The man had brought heather and small pine branches with him and these he laid on top of the pile. He examined some droppings left by black grouse before silently leaving. That evening from the top of another tree the squirrel watched a pine marten cross the clearing, bound up to the pile and walk around it sniffing. Then she saw him mark the pile with his scent. She kept very still for pine martens were good climbers and sometimes ate squirrels, but after inspecting the wide area of bare ground he turned towards another part of the forest to hunt.

The following day-break she watched the man transform the pile into a low mound, weaving the heather and pine branches into the netting. He attached a shiny round disc, facing the clearing, then left before black grouse, four cocks, their wings whirring, flew in and stationed themselves separately around the bare ground – which was their 'lek' where they displayed each spring. One cock, hissing 'chuwee' jumped on top of the man-made mound, and displayed by leaping up and down. The squirrel turned her back on the noisy birds and returned to her young in the dray. She knew that it was almost time for them to emerge and nibble young shoots already bursting.

Asleep with them that night, she didn't see the wildcat with its short striped bushy tail pad softly across the clearing, but the pine

marten did and agilely climbed the nearest tree! But no one saw the man and a companion arrive long before sun-up, remove the shiny disc and one crawl inside the mound. The squirrel merely saw a shadowy man leaving, and as this was now so commonplace, she got on with seeking out suitable shoots near the dray to introduce her young to later.

Pre-dawn was heralded by the whirring of wings as the four black grouse cocks arrived, calling 'chuwee' to proclaim their territories on the lekking ground. The squirrel heard their 'rookooing' sounds as they danced in solitary small circles, two dominant cocks claiming the centre ground. As dawn broke, greyhens arrived, walking the perimeter of the ground pretending to feed. Their presence excited the cocks who commenced wing flapping, jumping vertically six feet above the ground accompanied by a hissing 'shishoo'. The two dominant cocks jousted together, each vying to out-dance and out-jump the other in order to attract a greyhen to mate, but so preoccupied were they that they didn't notice a lesser male mate with a greyhen at the edge of the ground! Grabbing her neck feathers he'd opportunistically climbed on to her back. Then another greyhen approached one of the dominant cocks and whilst they mated his rival was challenged by a subordinate male. This contender stood erect, hissing, and flapping his wings, and was answered in the same way. Then the two ran at each other uttering a high-pitched 'grrrr', aiming to confront each other near the edge of their territories, but the contender over-ran the invisible boundary and was immediately attacked. Feet and beaks were soon entangled and feathers flying; the noise they made obliterating muffled clicking noises from the mound. After a two minute joust the victor jumped triumphantly on top of the mound, dancing in a final display that was cut short when a fox was sighted. Immediately all the black grouse became silent and still, necks outstretched. As the fox approached they flew back to their roosts in the forest.

The squirrel watched as the fox warily approached the unusual mound that 'clicked', he sniffed the canvas recognising pine marten and human scent. Rapidly retreating he disappeared into the forest. Day had dawned as the squirrel coaxed her three youngsters out of the dray and on to a branch. She showed them how to hold and nibble young green shoots. Used to the man now, she paid little attention as he folded up his hide, stuffing all but his camera into his bag.

Standing still he focused his lens on her tree, rapidly clicking. She knew he wasn't a threat but when his companion returned she shrank down against the branch, showing her youngsters how to react to danger.

As they left the man said – 'The lek was fantastic! I got some amazing shots before a black cock jumped on top of the hide and danced on my head! But I reckon my best photo will be of a red squirrel with a most magnificent tail.'

A NIGHT IN SPRINGTIME

In her warm bracken-lined chamber, deep underground, the sow badger sniffed cool night air wafting down the main tunnel. The heady scent of bluebells, titillating her sensitive nostrils throughout the day was replaced by damp night time smells of spring woodland. Vibrations shook the sandy galleries of the badger sett and muffled sounds echoed along the maze of tunnels. The sow knew her unwelcome neighbour, the vixen, was awake and scratching her mangy fur. It wouldn't be long before the vixen and her cubs would be outside in the dark wood too.

The sow nudged her three slumbering cubs awake. Well grown at ten weeks old, with thick wiry grey coats, they had learnt to follow her through the tunnels to the wide entrance hole under the big oak. For the past few nights they had played on the ancient excavation mound outside the sett but last night she'd led them along a track through the steep deciduous woodland, then home by a back entrance. But tonight, with their growing appetites, they were ready to forage for solid food.

She pushed them away as they nuzzled for milk, and leaving the cosy breeding chamber, climbed the narrow sloping tunnel. They followed, jostling where it widened at special passing places, detouring briefly to explore empty chambers. She inspected an upper chamber lined with dry grass and woodrush, knowing the musty bedding should be replaced. Her cubs were growing bigger so it wasn't long till her mate demanded his return to the sett. The boar had visited occasionally since the cub's birth but she'd driven him away because his amorous rough and tumble play could have killed the tiny cubs. Now the young boar and two sow cubs were ready to meet their social group, – including their father. Near the entrance the acrid smell of fox assailed her acute nose, an unpleasant reminder that the 'squatters' unsavoury quarters must be cleaned, once the vixen and her family departed.

The foxes were playing noisily near their hole, – four rangy cubs squabbling over a discarded bone, and the vixen rolling to relieve a flea itch. The sow knew this unguarded activity meant no men and dogs lurked in the wood. Her long-tailed neighbour was more skittish than she, but even so the sow cautiously sampled the air. The pungence of fox mingled with fresh budding woodland and a trace of wood smoke drifting from the farmhouse on the hill top. The sows limited eyesight took in dark trees against a full moon rising. The woodland shapes looked unchanged, there was no danger.

Instead of letting her cubs romp on the huge mound scraped from the sett over countless generations, she led them down the steep woodland track to fields. They were all hungry. Pastures where cows grazed and fields of winter wheat grew were profitable forage grounds. Her nose detected other animals that had passed that way recently, roe deer, rabbits, an old dog fox, and the musk of her sister with her two boar cubs born one week earlier than her own. All left a unique signature along the badger path.

Her sister's family occupied another sett locally, but her mate had been killed on the road that winter. The sow examined the dewy pasture where her sister's brood had foraged for insects and earthworms.

Further on she salivated over fat worms found on the cropped pasture. The sow showed her cubs how to sniff the damp vegetation, flattening it to 'snuffle holes' where any juicy worm or crunchy leatherjacket could be devoured. Later in the season, when snails and slugs became plentiful she would show them these too. She thought hungrily of wasps nests packed with succulent grubs and wild bee's honeycombs worth risking a sting or two, when the light evenings came. Looking at the leafless elder and hazel trees she knew, come autumn, their nuts and berries would provide rich food for her young if they survived the summer dry spell. In times of drought, earthworms, their staple food, buried so deep they couldn't be dug out. She hoped it would be a wetter summer than last when her two previous cubs died of starvation.

Trotting to the field edge she scraped a shallow hole, defecated, then dragged her rump along the ground, marking it with her musk. Cubs following, she inspected another 'dung pit' left by one of their group at the edge of their territory. Her cubs followed under a low tunnel of shrubby undergrowth into a ploughed field where winter wheat shoots glistened under the full moon. Reflecting silver rays on her rust-gold back was her sister, a rare erythristic badger, together with her normal grey-coloured cubs. They greeted by scenting each other with musk, the older cubs inquisitive, the younger shy. Eating a few worms and grubs together, the grey sow moved on again along a path across the field, where, smelling rabbits in the hedgerow she discovered a recently gouged hole where a nursery of baby rabbits had been devoured. Only deep claw marks, trampled vegetation and the unmistakeable musk of her mate remained.

Baby rabbits were too large for her cubs to eat, but at the years end when turned out from the sett, they would need to know survival tricks. Calling them to follow, she inspected the rabbit run where the farmer sometimes left snares. But her mate had beaten her and from a tightly drawn snare dangled the inside-out skin of a large rabbit. Nothing edible remained, so instead she led them to a dew pond where she demonstrated how to pounce on the croaking frogs.

A screeching barn owl, and chained dogs yapping on the hill top, made her turn for home, cubs following closely, still unsure of themselves and obedient to her commands. In the pasture she was joined by her red-haired sister and family also on their way home. Climbing the woodland track the grey sow picked up a musk trail, and knowing who awaited them at the sett she was prepared for her mate's amorous rush as he pounced upon her playfully. Then he inspected his offspring, nudging them roughly with his nose. The sow noticed the vixen slink back with her cubs, halting to watch warily. The boar, in uninhibited display, initiated a playful musking session. Over a wide area in front of the mound a roly-poly game ensued, all tangled together in age-old family play. The sow watched the vixen slip back down the hole. With the boar back, she knew it wouldn't be long before her neighbour moved on – to find somewhere quieter to live.

A HARD DAYS WORK

The short June night lightened to grey beyond rounded summits of the Southern Uplands. Woken by the shrill cry of a vixen in the valley below, the female short-eared owl ruffled her feathers. A cool breeze whispered through stiff young spruce trees, and lambs on the bare hills bleated to their mothers. Under the owl's narrow reddish-brown and fawn 40cm long wings, two chicks snuggled drowsily, whilst beneath her chest four smaller chicks and one egg, still incubating, lay warm in the shallow grass-lined nest. As dawn silhouetted eastern hill tops, she saw her mate perched in his slanting posture, on the forestry fence-post close by.

Establishing his territory in March, he'd selected the young forestry plantation and moorland for its abundant vole population. A rival male secured another part of the plantation and the treeless hill top. His mate had flown north in April from the English estuary where she'd overwintered, and on reaching the Southern Uplands, had been courted by him. Slightly smaller, with grey-brown streaked feathers, he had attracted her attention by flight display over his territory. Gliding on outspread wings, booming 'hoo hoo hoo hoo', he'd dropped like a stone from a height of 7 metres clapping his wings together loudly. Interested, she'd flown closer and he'd wooed her with his low flying zig-zag flight and wing clapping. When she'd responded with a high pitched 'keerrik', and begged for food, their partnership began.

Choosing a nest site among the young conifers they mated a week after pairing. The mixture of heather, rush, and grass on the forestry ridges made good nest cover and because there was an abundance of small mammals and moorland birds for food, a clutch of seven white eggs were laid over two weeks. Now more than a month had elapsed, her mate feeding her whilst she barely left the nest except for occasional flights with him when he lured her away with food. Now their two oldest chicks were already showing interest in wandering from the nest.

Tucking in stray nest grass, and shuffling with hungry anticipation, she examined the empty vole larder next to the nest. Her mate, alert on his perch, focused on tufted moorland grass nearby. Launching from the post he dropped to the grass, killing his victim before flying nest-wards, a vole dangling from his feet. Despite her own needs she took it and tore the tiny mammal into pieces to feed to her young, whilst he departed in search of more prey. With acute hearing and excellent eyesight he quickly killed a young pipit, spreading his wings fiercely he waited to ensure the small bird was dead. Successful every four or five times that he pounced, he safeguarded his kills from marauding crows and buzzards by this defensive behaviour. Calling softly 'hoo hoo hoo hoo' he brought this kill to the nest, returning a few minutes later with another plump vole that she fed, whole, to her oldest chick, now 14 days old.

The sun rose and the day warmed. Alighting by a small burn, he stood in the shallow flow flicking water over his feather. Shaking head and wings he preened for a few minutes before returning to his task. His rival quartering his own hill top, brought food to his mate, still incubating a full clutch of eggs.

In the plantation the two oldest chicks had scrambled from the nest and lay, separately, a short distance off, concealed in long grass. The female maintained contact, calling softly to them whilst ripping shreds of flesh from a shrew to feed the rest of her brood. Two dead voles lay stored in the larder. Her hunger assuaged by eating remnants of kills, she nevertheless pecked at a beetle crawling by her nest, gulping it down. Her mate flew in with more food, but stimulated by soft shrieking from his two large offspring, and the sight of their heads outstretched skywards, he dropped to the ground, feeding one instead.

Whilst seeking food for the other he spied a forester striding up the hillside examining the trees. Bounding ahead of him was a dog. As the dog intruded dangerously close to the nest the male clapped his wings and flew at the intruder. Swooping with talons outspread he struck the dog a glancing blow on its head. It turned tail, yelping. Alerted, the man strode straight towards the nest. The male short-eared owl, in fake injury display, tried to lure him away, flying around his head shrieking and crashing to the ground where he laid with wings outspread, head lolling from side to side. Undeterred the man found the nest where the female, eyes closed amidst their enlarging circle of dark feathers, and ear tufts raised to increase her threatening appearance, sat erect and immobile. Harrying the man's head, the male drove the forester away, flying just above him until he reached his territorial boundary. Soaring around the hill top his rival watched, concerned.

During this danger the chicks crouched amongst concealing grass tufts. Now safe, their mother called them as she shifted gently, for her last egg was hatching. If the weather stayed fair and voles numerous then their entire brood might survive the fledgling stage. If bad weather struck then this last chick and its closest sibling might be eaten by the others if food became scarce. Tomorrow another chick would leave the nest in daylight, isolating itself to increase its survival chances. Softly calling 'hoo hoo hoo', the male flew in, transferring prey from talons to mouth before he landed. A threat to their young had been averted, and for the time being food was plentiful.

It was twilight when the dog fox, rustling through rushes, alerted the male's attention. His day had been long, protecting and incessantly hunting for his mate and chicks. Again danger threatened. Before the fox was close he struck, swooping down in the dim light. His mate stiffened in upright posture on her nest, guarding now seven chicks. Dive-bombing again and again the fox finally capitulated, rolling on its back with legs submissively in the air. Aroused by the commotion the rival male was joined by its mate, and they flew low together seeing the threat. Looking back over his shoulder the dog fox slunk away down the hillside. Assured that danger was past, the male short-eared owl returned to his perch on the forestry post, whilst his mate settled comfortably over her brood as twilight faded and the evening star appeared in the clear night sky.

MONARCH OF THE MOUNTAINS

Standing on his mountain crag the regal stag gazed upon his kingdom. The Highland glens were shrouded in early morning mist from which rocky peaks appeared like islands. Head pointing into the wind he breathed deeply, his senses no less diminished despite his advanced years. He smelt hinds and their calves on slopes far below and the pungency of stags closer by. He had left the herd and with his companion, a five year old stag, had spent the summer's night under the summit of a Cairngorm peak. The rising sun warmed his rust-red flank and he shook himself, his moulting coat shedding course hair. He knew the other stags would emerge above the mist into the sunlight soon.

His 'squire' following, he took a narrow track between bare rocks where a ptarmigan nested, down to a sheltered hollow where tender summer grass and heather grew amongst lichen and moss. Hunger gnawed and he knew next winter's strength lay in the lush summer herbage so bending his heavily antlered head, he browsed, grasping heather tips, jerking upwards to bite with long yellow teeth. One incisor was missing, and he chewed rhythmically, the sharp ridges of his molars grinding the tiny leaves.

His companion, one of many grandsons, stood alert as stags appeared from the eastern corrie where they'd spent the night. Only when they'd started feeding did his squire feed. The old stag had once been a 'squire; lower at the shoulder, shorter of body, later boasting a black stream from forehead to rump showing his prime condition. His teeth had been white then and his hooves smaller and trim. Now he ate steadily, filling his huge stomach.

The sun rose higher lifting the last shreds of mist. He knew the day would be hot and was glad to be high up in a breeze with few flies to bother them, whilst the hinds would be pestered by warble flies and midges on their lower grazing. Feeling a tick crawling amongst his facial hair he rubbed his cheek against a rock. He was thirsty and the high burns had dried this fine summer spell so he led his companion down to a lochan beside which tiny alpine flowers and hardy club-moss grew in soil-filled pockets between circles of frost-heaved stones. The stag recalled times he'd been there in summer storms, sheltering in the lee of crags from gusting winds and lashing hail. Wild and inhospitable most of the year, today a lark was singing, and there was scarcely a ripple on the lochan.

The fragrance of fresh water assailed his sensitive nostrils. Both deer broke into a trot; the squire's head erect, the old stag's nodding slightly. Drinking deeply from the shallows where glossy fat tadpoles swam, he quenched his thirst. His companion watched, turning windward to listen, before he too drank. A pair of golden eagles nesting on a precipitous ledge nearby lazily quartered the peak, slide-slipping the air space over another corrie, before soaring on the up-draught.

The sun was hot, the sky deep blue when they found a midday resting place. Rejecting scarred earthy ledges where he'd often ruminated, the old stag chose the corrie edge where the mountainside fell away to a long glacial valley. Silhouetting himself with noble indifference he cudded confidently, whilst his companion, away from the edge, remained vigilant.

Far below in the grassy glen a red car passed grazing sheep on its way to a car park. The stag watched it, grey to him, remembering the time when he'd first encountered such a creature. It had been winter and he a young 'staggie' a little over a year old with his first small antlers. The herd, hinds as well as stags, had moved from exposed winter grazing, invading a forestry plantation to shelter amongst spruce and larch – to strip bark. Lingering on the road he'd been dazzled by headlights, narrowly escaping when the car suddenly braked. His mother, matriarch of the hinds, had butted him when he rejoined them and he'd not forgotten her punishment, avoiding cars after that! He drowsed in the sunshine remembering the lessons he'd learnt before he'd left the hinds to rear their new calves, whilst he joined the stags.

A breeze swayed tussocks at the corrie edge conjuring up more cycles of years as he'd grown to maturity. Each year he'd grown a new set of antlers, with more points successively and a stronger head to proudly bear them. Finally a supreme twelve pointer, he'd risen to dominate the herd as a 'Royal' stag. At seventeen years he had now survived longer than others. The sweet smell of peat titillated his nostrils and he recalled rolling in the peaty wallow, blackening his coat and spreading musk from glands under his eyes for the hinds to smell during the rut.

Suddenly agitated, the young stag stood up, nervously trotting a few steps away. People from the car were slowly climbing the hill. Wearily getting to his feet the old stag shook his shaggy mane and followed heavily after. The heat, plus memories of the rutting wallow, made the old stag trace the peaty aroma to a boggy hollow where cotton grass and sedge grew. His skin itching, he rolled, shedding chunks of loose coat, revelling in the cool dampness. His squire waited his turn patiently.

A stronger breeze had risen by the time they took an ancient track across the heights to the far side where they could see Caledonian pine forest in a wider glen. Knowing where his favourite food, whortleberries, grew the old stag led on to a grassy level above hind territory from where he could see them with their spotted calves, lying cudding. There were about thirty of them, so well camouflaged that they looked like a scattering of brown lichen-covered rocks. Finding a few ripe whortleberries the stags nibbled whilst keeping a watchful eye on the rocky shoulder leading to the glen. The breeze blew with it human scent. The surer sighted young stag saw the hill-walkers first and turned tail showing his pale rump. Below, the watchful hinds had also seen the intruders and rapidly responded. In full flight they streamed like a brown waterfall over the edge of a steep slope to safety.

A red sun was sinking beyond western mountains when the two stags found their new night shelter. As the young stag lay down the old stag climbed a promontory. Bathed in its aura the stag gazed westwards – a monarch indeed with such a kingdom at his feet.

JOURNEY'S END

Far below the young barnacle goose could see land. It was the first he'd seen since leaving the east coast of Greenland. Older geese in his skein called in a rapid yap-yapping sound at the sight. This new land looked so different. Whereas Greenland was grey-green in places near the sea, but stark white inland, the land below was a mosaic of greens and browns, with glittering shades of rosy gold where lochans reflected the October dawn. It was an island, the largest of a string of isles extending southwards. Tired and hungry, the green food seen far below enticing, he wanted to stop beating his aching wings and glide downwards, but the other geese, following their leader, showed no sign of descending.

He had been flying endlessly without rest. Other skeins of migrating geese flew parallel to them. Sometimes they overlapped, their V's linked as W's, sometimes they lost their V-shape as stragglers tried desperately to catch up. One old female had not made it. He had fallen behind once but his mother encouraged him on, falling back with him, urging him on with strong wing beats and sharp sounding barks. Flying had become easier once they'd met wind that had lifted them and helped them fly across the vast, empty ocean. This same wind was still blowing them southeast. He could feel the strong air current beneath him, cold air sleeking his lavender-grey breast feathers, cooling his long black neck, arching his fine primary feathers at the tips of his long black and white striped wings.

They were a fine formation, his mother just ahead of him, her white rump and black tail feathers covering her folded black feet. From the corner of his small dark eye he could see his sisters behind, halfway down the right side of the V, whilst at the apex of the skein his father led the way. Several other geese made up their formation numbering two-dozen or so birds. His own family numbered five, although it should have totalled six. Now, at only a few months old, he recalled his earliest days in the nest high on the Greenland cliff.

The nest was warm and comfortable, made of fluffy down feathers mixed with bits of moss and lichen. He'd shared it with three greyish-white eggs, before they too hatched. He recalled his mother settling herself gently over him and the eggs that eventually became his brother and sisters. His father at this time stood patiently nearby, guarding against marauders.

He'd been the first, a brother gosling second. Once their downy feathers had dried they'd instinctively left the cup-shaped nest to feed. Their father had encouraged them along the precipitous rocky ledge and they followed, trustingly jumping to flat footholds below. At one difficult place they had to leap, and he'd tumbled quite a height, a bouncing ball of fluff, before scrambling to his feet at the edge of a deep ravine. His unlucky brother missed the landing spot and a predatory gull swooped into the ravine after him, whilst his father barked and beat his wings, – but there was nothing he could do. Shepherded onwards he arrived safely at a marsh on the green tundra where geese and goslings pecked vegetation with short black beaks. His father showed him how to eat, what was good and what was not. His mother and two sisters eventually joined them.

Long summer nights when the sun never set, tender shoots, catkins, roots and seeds to eat, and myriads of buzzing flies – that's what he remembered. Life had consisted of eating. His down quickly disappeared as real feathers grew through and he'd learnt to preen, parting the tiny barbules of each shaft and coating them with a fine layer of waterproofing oil. In line with his sisters, he'd followed his parents to a lake where after initial surprise at encountering deep water, he'd paddled furiously, the webs of his black feet spread wide. Here his parents had shown him how to nibble worms from the muddy bottom and to catch small crustaceans. Sometimes the lake was full of other geese, not all of them Barnacles. On several occasions they had taken off yapping vociferously, exploding in a kaleidoscopic riot of monochrome, their fear-induced wing beats drumming the air. This happened when an arctic fox pounced on an injured goose hobbling at the lake's edge, and when a polar bear splashed into the water surprising them. Despite the airspace filling with a confusion of ascending wings, he discovered that they became a homogeneous entity, winging as one vast flock, to a safer area.

Now those same geese were en-route to their over-wintering grounds. He could see thin black skeins far ahead and to both sides. Leaving their summer breeding grounds was a shared decision. He'd been aware of a strange stirring within himself, and restlessness in the older geese. Continuous daylight became punctuated by twilight, then short nights that gradually lengthened and grew colder. The arctic sun sank lower in the sky each day and older geese on trial flights tended to fly south-eastwards. His parents who had nurtured him and his sisters for seven weeks of summer reacted similarly, whilst he was innately attracted in the same direction. He'd been proud when his wing feathers had grown long enough for him to join the flock on these trial flights. An excitement was growing within him. When his father and mother finally took off, he and his sisters joined them together with other barnacle geese in their vicinity. Others ranged out over the tundra took flight also, creating their own V-shaped formations.

Now, hunger gnawed and his breast and wing muscles ached. The autumn sun was at its highest when his father changed direction slightly, leaving the last of the island chain, to head in a more easterly direction. Every barnacle goose followed suit. Looking down to his left the young goose saw two low isles before a larger mountainous island, behind which spread a vast expanse of mountains. They flew on, dropping progressively lower. Ahead he saw a small island and three high peaks of a larger island beyond. The red sun was dropping back into the sea, the western sky every hue of gold when he saw bare rock reflecting the sunset on west-facing slopes. The skein straggled slightly towards this mountainous isle and he felt desperate. Surely they weren't going to that barren place? Then away to his right he saw a bigger, flat, green island. The older geese in the skein began yapping, barking joyful calls that had him yapping excitedly back, as they descended and circled noisily. Below were verdant fields dotted with sheep. Other pastures were speckled with thousands of geese. They were not the first to arrive. Coasting down on bowed wings, dropping his legs but tilting his body backwards to beat his wings in a reverse thrust, he landed on rich pastures close to a sea loch. The air was full of the sounds of barnacle geese, ecstatic that their long journey was at last over. The place was amazing! He was surrounded by food! He watched his exhausted parents and sisters looking around at the vast gathering, then, they lowered their heads to tear hungrily at the lush grass. Something deep inside told him, that this at last, was his journey's end.

DISCOVER MORE SCOTTISH WILDLIFE AT THESE WEBSITES

Ged Connelly – a naturalist since boyhood, is a tireless wildlife photographer. He worked closely with the writer detailing much wildlife information used in the stories, and is mentioned in 'A Hard Day's Work' – the story about short eared owls and in 'The Red Squirrel's Tale' – in which a Black grouse cock really did 'dance' on his head! Ged Connelly gives illustrated wildlife talks, is involved in Scottish wildlife protection, and is a surveyor for wind farm location. *Badger, Red fox, Red deer, Red squirrel, Mountain hare, Red kite, Black grouse, Short-eared owl, Snow bunting, Crossbill, Mute swan, Great crested grebe, Shag, Gannet, Puffin, Fulmar, Dotterel, Oystercatcher, Redshank, Butterflies, Scottish landscapes.* **www.gedconnellyimages.co.uk**

Pete Cairns – **www.northshots.com** *Osprey, Scottish Wildcats.*

Forestry Commission Scotland – **www.forestry.gov.uk/pictures** *Capercaillie, Pipistrelle bat, Peregrine, Grey heron,* John MacTavish – *Black throated diver, Roe deer.*

Jenny Green – **www.photo-opportunities.com** *Common seals, Rock pool, Stags head, Limpets.*

Jeremy Hastings – **www.islaybirding.co.uk** *Barnacle Geese, Chough, Whooper Swans.*

MacDuff Marine Aquarium – **www.marine-aquarium.com** *Anemone, Cod, Lumpsucker, Ray.*

Northern Light Charters – **www.northernlight-uk.com** Mark Henrys – *Minke Whale. Guests of Northern Light Charters,* Richard Crossen – *Greater Black-back Gull, Eider Duck,* Nick Clark – *Conger Eel,* Steve Cloke – *Wrasse,* Dawn Menzies – *Orca,* Sheila Saltmarsh – *Common Dolphin,* Graham Savage – *Great Skua,* Michael Steciuk – *Kittiwake, Arctic Tern,* Paul Webster – *Basking Shark.*

Charlie Phillips Images – **www.charliephillipsimages.co.uk** *Bottlenose Dolphin, Harbour porpoise.*

R.S.P.B. Photo Library – **www.rspb-images.com** Sue Tranter – *Raven,* Chris Gomersall – *Red-Throated Diver and Great Northern Diver.*

Scottish Wildlife Trust – **www.swt.org.uk** *Crested Tit, Curlew,* Norman Tait – *Greenshank,* Michael Davison – *Osprey, Pine marten.*

Scottish Association for Marine Science – **www.sams.ac.uk** *Plaice,* Hugh Brown – *Blenny*

The Scottish Wildcat Association – **www.scottishwildcats.co.uk** Peter Cairns – *Wildcats*

Steve Reddick – **www.highlandwildlifesafaris.co.uk** *Corncrake.*

Steve Sankey – **www.orcadianwildlife.co.uk** *Grey Seal.*

Jerry Sutton – **www.jerry-suttonphotography.co.uk** *Otters.*

Wild Scotland – **www.wild-scotland.co.uk** *Hen Harrier, Ptarmigan, Red Grouse, Guillemot.*

Turus Mara – **www.turusmara.com** *Tour Boat.*

Scottish Viewpoint – **www.scottishviewpoint.com** – *Scottish salmon*

Visit Scotland Wildlife – **www.visitscotland.com/wildlife**

Chris Gomersall photography – *Sea eagle, Golden eagle, Manx shearwater.*

Craigmore Publications thank all photographers, both professional and amateur, and organisations for their generosity in donating images to 'Discover Scotland's Wildlife'. Clara Govier and Alan Anderson of the Scottish Wildlife Trust, Caroline Warburton of Wild Scotland, Laura Stewart of Forestry Commission Scotland, Hannah Thompson of Northern Light Charters, David Sexton RSPB Isle of Mull, Steve Piper of Coffee Films, Susan MacKinnon of Clunie Group Ltd, Oban, and Nick Jones are thanked for all their help, input, and support in producing this publication.